# WIMBLEDON VILLAGE
## *a history told through its street names*

by

## Neal Ransome

*To Jennifer*

*Neal Ransome*

## Wimbledon Society Museum Press

The Wimbledon Society, Registered Charity (No 1164261), was founded in 1903 and has had its present name since 1982. (Originally the John Evelyn Club, it was known as the John Evelyn Society from 1949–82.) Its main objectives are to preserve Wimbledon's amenities and natural beauty, study its history, and ascertain that urban development is sympathetic and orderly.

Published by the Wimbledon Society Museum Press

Sales and distribution: Museum of Wimbledon,
22 Ridgway, London SW19 4QN
Open 2.30–5.00pm Saturday and Sunday. Admission free

Go to www.wimbledonmuseum.org.uk to purchase online

ISBN 978-0-9576151-9-9

Printed and bound in Great Britain by Intype Libra Ltd,
Units 3–4 Elm Grove Industrial Estate, Elm Grove, Wimbledon,
London SW19 4HE (www.intypelibra.co.uk).

Cover: Postcard of High Street, Wimbledon, early 20th century, published by The Collector's Publishing Company, London, reproduced by permission of London Borough of Merton.

Cover Design: Nigel Davies

Title page illustration: Postcard of Ridgway, Wimbledon, at the entrance to Wright's Alley, c1908, published by The Collector's Publishing Company, London, from the author's collection.

# CONTENTS

# PREFACE AND ACKNOWLEDGEMENTS

This book is the product of a slightly obsessive interest in the origins of the street names of Wimbledon Village, nurtured over many years of living in the area. It is based on a combination of both primary and secondary research. Secondary sources are listed in a bibliography at the back of the book. Primary research has been conducted at the Surrey History Centre, the Merton Heritage and Local Studies Centre and the Museum of Wimbledon. I have also made use of internet-based resources. The pleasure, to me at least, of researching Wimbledon's street names has been that it has drawn me into a deeper exploration of Wimbledon's local history. This book, therefore, goes beyond the origins of the Village's street names to comment on the histories behind those names. It provides a brief history of the residential development of Wimbledon Village and a patchwork of the characters and incidents that have combined to make up the rich tapestry of Wimbledon's past.

I would like to thank the following individuals and groups of people for their direct and indirect assistance in the creation of this book; the authors listed in this book's bibliography, with a particular acknowledgement of the major contribution made to our knowledge of Wimbledon's history by the late Richard Milward; the staff and volunteers of the Surrey History Centre, the Merton Heritage and Local Studies Centre and the Museum of Wimbledon, and in particular Sarah Gould and Dr Pamela Greenwood, for assisting my research in their archives; Charles Toase and Cyril Maidment of the Wimbledon Society

Local History Group for reviewing and commenting on the historical content of this book; Cyril Maidment again for permission to make use of maps created by him in the design of maps included in this book; the National Portrait Gallery, London, for permission to use images from its collection; the London Borough of Merton for permission to use images from the Merton Memories Photographic Archive (www.merton. gov.uk/memories); the many individuals with whom I communicated in the process of gathering explanations for some of the obscurer street names in the Village; my wife, Patricia Lovell, and my sister, Heather Ransome, for reviewing and editing the text; Cassandra Taylor and other members of the Committee of the Museum of Wimbledon for their decision to publish this book; Nigel Davies for designing the book's cover and maps; Kevin O'Neil, the Museum's Publications Officer, for his invaluable support in driving forward the process of converting a raw word document into a published book.

I am grateful to all of these people for their help in the production of this book. Any remaining errors or omissions are, of course, my own.

I am certain that the explanations and histories recounted in this book are not complete in every respect. If any readers have any additional information on the origins of any of Wimbledon's street names I would be delighted to hear from them. I can be contacted via my e-mail address: neal.ransome@gmail.com.

# LIST OF ILLUSTRATIONS

# INTRODUCTION

The streets covered in this book are restricted to the ward of Wimbledon Village, as defined by Merton Council. This is partly to keep this book to manageable proportions, but principally because Wimbledon's history prior to the 19th century was exclusively focused on the Village area. The Village ward occupies Merton's north-west corner. The boundary runs up the west side of Wimbledon Common along the route of Beverley Brook, cuts across the Common via the windmill and continues along Queensmere Road to the centre of Wimbledon Park by the lake. From the park it zigzags down Church Road and across Home Park Road, Arthur Road and Leopold Road before returning to Wimbledon Hill Road via Lake Road and

## Chart showing the number of new streets developed each period

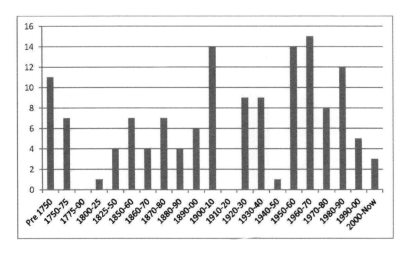

Belvedere Drive. It then skips across Draxmont and up Sunny-side to the Ridgway, before running down Cottenham Park Road and along Coombe Lane back to Beverley Brook.

There are currently 141 streets in the Wimbledon Village area. Fewer than 20 were in existence in the year 1800. Like the rest of the country, Wimbledon experienced a major population boom in the 19th century, and this precipitated the creation of 33 new roads. The rate of population growth slowed in the 20th century, but the demand for new housing did not abate. A total of 87 new streets were developed in the Village in the 20th century, and this was despite the fact that only one new road was developed in the two decades dominated by the two World Wars. The extent of development in both the 19th and 20th centuries would have been greater still had some heroic conservation campaigns not been fought to preserve Wimbledon's green spaces. The rate of development does at last appear to have slowed down, with only three new streets having been laid out since the turn of this century.

## Chart showing the origin of street names by category

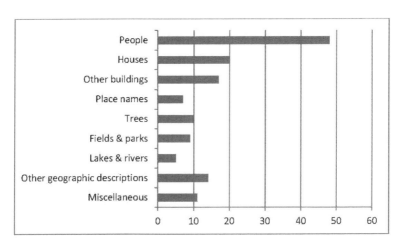

One third (48) of the streets in the Village are named after individuals. All but five of these individuals have a direct association with Wimbledon. The five exceptions are two members of the royal family (Queen Victoria's sons Arthur and Leopold), one American president (Lincoln), one Cardinal (Wolsey) and the medieval folk hero Robin Hood. It probably isn't a surprise that politicians and statesmen appear most frequently in the list of individuals commemorated, accounting for 19 street names. Royalty and other members of the aristocracy account for a further four streets. Excluding Robin Hood, five names acknowledge public benefactors (Atkinson, Holland, Marryat, Rydon and Thurstan). Other professions recognised include one soldier (Murray), one teacher (Lancaster) and, disregarding Cardinal Wolsey, one cleric (Haygarth). At present, and this may be something for Merton Council to address in the naming of future streets, not a single street in the Village can definitively be said to commemorate a woman. The closest candidates are Marryat Place and Road, which are named after local residents Joseph and Charlotte Marryat. Although several of the individuals may have had mixed parentage, not least Queen Victoria's two sons, only four of them can definitively be described as foreigners (Calonne, Cannizaro, Lincoln and Charlotte Marryat).

A quarter (37) of the streets in the Village are named after houses or other buildings. Twenty are named after houses. Almost invariably these streets have been laid out in the grounds of the houses whose names they commemorate. The one exception is Allington Close, which was named after a house in Merton Park. Although a few of these houses survive, the majority were demolished in the process of developing the streets which bear their names. Of the 17 other buildings referenced in street names eight relate to religious buildings, including two priories and one abbey which have no link with Wimbledon (Dunstall, Ellerton and Newstead). There are also

11

references to two schools, one long since closed (Beltane), and one extant but no longer in Wimbledon (Rokeby).

A further quarter (38) of the streets have names which refer either to trees or to geographic features associated with these streets. There are ten streets named after trees (including Copse Hill but excluding Woodhayes Road). Of these ten, four refer to cedar trees (Cedar Court, Cedarland Terrace, Cedar Park Gardens and High Cedar Drive). All of these streets are recent (post 1960) and cedars are clearly held in high regard by residential property developers. Nine streets refer to fields and parks, and five to lakes and rivers. The remaining streets in this geographic category generally have prosaic descriptive names such as North View and Westside Common (hereafter Westside).

Of the remaining 18 streets in the Village seven are named after places. Six of these places are elsewhere in England, and one, Wimbledon Hill Road, is the only street in the Village to include a reference to Wimbledon in its name. The final 11 street names are a miscellany. They include two references to ships (Barham and Hood), two references to novels (Cranford and Windy Ridge) and one reference to a bird (Peregrine). This category also includes a small handful of roads where developers and estate agents have clearly influenced the selection of names which can best be described as poetic. These streets include Haven Close and Royal Close.

Exactly a third (47) of the streets in the Village are described as 'roads'. This most prosaic description tended to be the default naming option prior to the Second World War, but has fallen out of favour since then, with no residential 'roads' created since Lindisfarne Road in 1932. 'Closes' and 'places', the majority of them cul-de-sac, account for another 32 streets, testifying to the Village's status today as a garden suburb. In contrast to 'roads' only one of the 18 'closes' in the Village was named prior to the Second World War (Allington Close). A further seven descriptions are used in the names of at least

## Chart showing street names by type

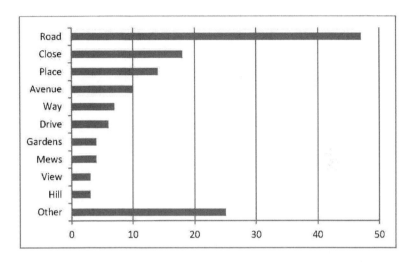

three streets. The remaining 25 streets in the Village share 23 separate titles. The Village has only one 'lane' (Coach House Lane), only one 'square' (Belvedere Square) and, fittingly, only the High Street is entitled as a 'street'.

Of the 141 streets in the Village, the explanations for the names of 136 can be arrived at with a high degree of certainty. In summarising these explanations in the body of this book I have given greater emphasis to those which have a historical background, and I have generally expanded the explanations to tell some of the history of Wimbledon and its residents. There is sometimes less scope for expanding upon the stories of those streets whose names are purely descriptive. There are three streets named after individuals where the explanation for the choice of name is somewhat speculative (Alan, Carnegie and St Aubyn), and two streets named after places (Alfreton and Welford) where, despite the fact that they are relatively recent creations, the rationale for the naming appears to be unknown. It is a particular frustration that two of these five mystery streets appear right at the start of the alphabetic list that follows. I hope that you will be able to get beyond them.

# A BRIEF HISTORY OF WIMBLEDON VILLAGE

Others, in particular Richard Milward, have written comprehensive histories of Wimbledon. The bibliography at the end
of this book gives details of several of Richard Milward's
works, along with a number of other books that I have read and
relied upon in compiling this review of the Village's street
names. The purpose of this brief history is not to spread new
light on well-trodden ground, but to provide an overview of the
residential development of the Village that will give context to
some of the more detailed episodes of local history that are
described in the body of this book.

## Caesar's Camp

The geography of Wimbledon Village has two particular char-
acteristics that have made it an attractive location for human
settlement for many, many centuries. The first of these is its
position on the top of a hill, which will always have afforded
its residents a degree of protection, both against wild animals
and predatory humans. The second key feature is the natural
spring water that surfaces, or is accessible, at many points on
and around the Common.

   The most tangible evidence of Wimbledon's ancient history
is the remains of the hill-fort on the Common known as
Caesar's Camp. Relatively little is known about the origins of
this site, but we do know that neither Julius Caesar nor any
other Caesar played any part in its creation. It acquired the
name Caesar's Camp in the 1820s, and had previously been

known locally as The Rounds. The current best estimate is that the hill-fort was constructed in about 700BC, just as the Bronze Age turned into the Iron Age, approximately 650 years before Julius Caesar first landed in England, and 750 years before the Roman invasion. There is speculation that Wimbledon's hill-fort was one of a chain of similar forts running south of the Thames that were used as centres of trade.

Until 1875 Caesar's Camp still had ramparts that were 10 to 20 feet high. In that year the Camp fell victim to what has perhaps been the sorriest act of developmental vandalism in Wimbledon's history. The owner of Caesar's Camp and the surrounding land, which was then known as the Old Park to distinguish it from Wimbledon Park on the other side of the Common, was one John Sawbridge-Erle-Drax, MP. In the face of strong local opposition he agreed to let the land to a builder

*1. Caesar's Camp, c1930. (Photograph reproduced by permission of London Borough of Merton)*

who proposed to build houses on the site. His opponents were eventually successful in blocking plans to develop the land, but not before the ramparts of Caesar's Camp had been razed to the ground.

## The Medieval Era

There exists practically no tangible evidence of Wimbledon's history during the 1,700 years that passed between the construction of Wimbledon's hill-fort and the Norman invasion of England in 1066. From at least the eighth century Wimbledon was part of a much larger manor (a feudal area of land owned by a lord) centred on Mortlake and owned by the Archbishop of Canterbury. There is one reference in the Domesday Book of 1086 to a church which may have been the first church on the site of what is now St Mary's on Church Road, but beyond this there is no reference to Wimbledon as a settlement. The manor of Mortlake does get a mention in the Domesday Book, and at that date Wimbledon appears to have been no more than a satellite farm or 'grange'.

A quarter of a millennium later, there is evidence of a more substantial settlement in Wimbledon. We have from 1332 a list of Wimbledon householders required to pay tax to help fund Edward III's war in Scotland. There are 31 householders included on the list, and by deduction the Village's population as a whole might have numbered 200. Most of the population were congregated along what is today the High Street. There were three principal routes leading from the Village, one towards Merton (now Wimbledon Hill Road), one towards Putney (Parkside) and one towards Kingston (Ridgway and Copse Hill). These three routes still converge at the bottom of the High Street.

The remainder of the medieval era witnessed little further developmental activity in Wimbledon. This was the age of the bubonic plague, and it is likely that Wimbledon's population will have diminished over these years. In English history the end of the medieval era and the beginning of the modern age are generally defined by Henry VII's accession to the throne following the Battle of Bosworth in 1485. In Wimbledon's history the defining moment came shortly afterwards, in approximately 1500, with the building of the Old Rectory, Wimbledon's first brick and oldest surviving building.

## The Tudor Years

The Old Rectory is Wimbledon's best-kept secret, tucked away behind Church Road, just north of St Mary's Church. The building was probably commissioned by the then Archbishop of Canterbury, John Morton. The Archbishop and his successors did not have many years in which to benefit from the residence because in 1536 one of Morton's successors, Archbishop Thomas Cranmer, was obliged to transfer the lordship of Wimbledon, including ownership of the Old Rectory, to the Crown as part of the dismantling of the Church's power that accompanied Henry VIII's decision to break with Rome during his quest to divorce Catherine of Aragon and marry Anne Boleyn.

During the next few years the lordship of Wimbledon changed hands on several occasions as the political fortunes of assorted Tudor statesmen rose and fell. Initially, Henry VIII passed the lordship to his principal adviser, Thomas Cromwell. On Thomas's demise in 1540 the lordship passed back to the Crown, and in 1543 Henry VIII granted the estate to his sixth and final wife, Catherine Parr. On Catherine's death in 1548 (one year after the death of the King), the estate again reverted to the Crown, and bounced around for several more years until 1576 when Queen Elizabeth I granted the lordship to one of her court favourites, Sir Christopher Hatton (subsequently Lord Chancellor).

The Old Rectory had its finest hour during these turbulent

times when, in December 1546, Henry VIII was taken ill on a journey back to London and was compelled to lay up at the Old Rectory to recover. Henry made it back to London, but died the following month. Four years later, in 1550, the Old Rectory was leased as a country retreat by Sir William Cecil, later Lord Burghley, chief minister to Queen Elizabeth I.

The Old Rectory was the childhood home of Sir William's son, Sir Thomas Cecil. Sir Thomas's memories of growing up in Wimbledon must have been favourable, because in 1576 he purchased the lordship of Wimbledon from its latest owner, Sir Christopher Hatton. Whilst the area may have pleased Sir Thomas, the relative frugality of the Old Rectory apparently did not, and in 1588 (the year of England's naval victory over the Spanish Armada) Sir Thomas was responsible for building the first of Wimbledon's four great manor houses (Cecil House).

Cecil House was built at the top of what is now Home Park Road, with extensive views down the hill. In terms of scale it was closer to a palace than a house. This first manor house was, without doubt, the grandest building ever to have graced the Village. The construction of Cecil House marked the beginning of the slow decline (but not demise) of the Old Rectory. No longer Wimbledon's most prestigious residence, by 1720 the Old Rectory was known as the Old Laundry House, and some years later it was in use as a dairy.

The Tudor years ended with Elizabeth I's death in 1603. For Wimbledon, the final highlight of the Tudor era had taken place four years earlier in 1599 when Sir Thomas had the honour of entertaining Elizabeth I and her retinue for three days in his splendid new manor house.

## Cecil House and the 17th century

Cecil House remained the most important building in Wimbledon throughout the 17th century. In 1616 Sir Thomas played

*2. Sir Thomas Cecil, 1st Earl of Exeter, c1595. (Stipple engraving by Robert Cooper, after William Derby, after Cornelius Johnson, published in 1825 by Harding, Triphook & Lepard, © National Portrait Gallery, London)*

host to Elizabeth I's successor, James I. In the following year, Sir Thomas commissioned a survey of his Wimbledon estate which recorded that the Village consisted of 45 houses occupied by 230 inhabitants. In 1623, on Sir Thomas's death, the lordship of the manor passed to his son, Edward Cecil, 1st Viscount Wimbledon. Cecil House survived an explosion in 1628 when some maids (whose fate is not recorded) mistook a barrel of gunpowder for soap powder. When Edward Cecil died in 1638 without a male heir not only did his title lapse, but the lordship was sold back to Charles I, who gave Cecil House to his wife, Queen Henrietta Maria. The Queen commissioned court architect Inigo Jones to modernise the building. Before she had time to enjoy the benefits of his work the English Civil War intervened, her husband lost his head, and the Crown was stripped of many of its possessions, including Cecil House. In 1649 the lordship and Cecil House were made over to the Cromwellian General, Sir John Lambert. Just as previous lords of the manor had entertained their king or queen at Cecil House, so Lambert played host to his head of state, the Lord Protector Oliver Cromwell.

The Interregnum was short-lived and, soon after Charles II was restored to the throne in 1660, his mother Henrietta Maria recovered Cecil House, and promptly sold it. During the next 50 years it was owned by two earls, the Earl of Bristol and the Earl of Danby, before being sold in 1717 to a wealthy French-born Huguenot financier, Sir Theodore Jannsen (subsequently 1st Baronet of Wimbledon). Jannsen found Cecil House to be outmoded and, shortly after he had acquired it, he razed it to the ground. Wimbledon's finest-ever house had stood for a mere 130 years.

While Cecil House was by far the most important building in Wimbledon Village throughout the 17th century, it did not remain the only substantial building. The Cecils had put Wimbledon on the map as a desirable place of residence within a few hours' ride from the centre of London. In the course of the 17th century a number of other wealthy individuals, predominantly London merchants rather than members of the landed classes ('new money' in modern parlance), commissioned substantial homes in and around the High Street.

The first of these new houses was the house subsequently

*3. Cecil House, c1678. (Engraving by J. Lee after Winstanley, published in 1811 by T. Cadell & W. Davies, from the collection of The Museum of Wimbledon)*

known as Eagle House, which Robert Bell built on the High Street in approximately 1613. In 1650 Thomas Hilliard built Claremont House just around the corner close to The Green, and in 1690 John Breholt, another Huguenot merchant, built what became the Old House just off the High Street on Church Road. In addition to these grand houses, there is plenty of other evidence of the High Street's status as the centre of a thriving community in the 17th century. Wimbledon's oldest pub (now the Dog & Fox, but then the Sign of my Lord's Arms) is referred to in a survey of 1617, and its first rival on the High Street, the Rose & Crown (then the Sign of the Rose) was built in approximately 1650.

## The gentrification of the Common and the development of Wimbledon's large estates

The development of Wimbledon Village in the first half of the Georgian era (from the accession of George I in 1714 to the death of George II in 1760) probably did more to determine its future shape and character than any other period. This period witnessed the construction of two new manor houses, the building of many of the major houses that now surround the Common, and the creation of several large estates which between them carved up most of the land within the bound-aries of the wider Village area.

Sir Theodore Jannsen, who had acquired the lordship in 1717 and subsequently demolished Cecil House, was not a newcomer to Wimbledon. In 1710 Jannsen is recorded as the first resident of another very fine house which was to play a large part in the future history and development of the Village. This house, which was situated at the very top end of the High Street (where Marryat Road now joins the High Street), was known as Wimbledon House. In 1720, like many Wimbledon residents to follow, Sir Theodore decided to upgrade, and he used the bricks of the demolished Cecil House to build the second of Wimbledon's four historic manor houses. The site that he chose for this house, which subsequently became known as Belvedere House, was located between what are now Alan and Highbury Roads. Sadly for Sir Theodore, he did not have long to enjoy his new manor house. As well as having been in 1694 a founder-member of the Bank of England, Sir Theodore was a director of the infamous South Sea Company. This company, which had been set up with a monopoly over trade in South America, had become the subject of massive investment speculation, including rampant insider dealing. When the company collapsed (the 'South Sea Bubble'), Jannsen and other directors were stripped of the majority of their fortunes to compensate ruined investors. Janssen was forced to sell Belvedere House and his lordship, although he was allowed to retain sufficient funds to retire to a more modest dwelling on Church Road.

The lordship of Wimbledon, and with it Belvedere House, was purchased by Sarah Churchill, Duchess of Marlborough. The Duchess, who had been Queen Anne's closest personal adviser in the early years of her reign, was one of the richest women in Europe, and wisely invested much of her fortune in property. This may have been why, some years after acquiring Belvedere House, she decided in 1733 to build Wimbledon's third manor house. This house, which became known as Marlborough House, was built just off Arthur Road, in what are now the grounds of Ricards Lodge School.

Sir Theodore and the Duchess were not the only people keeping architects and builders busy in Wimbledon in the first half of the 18th century. This was the period when many of the fine houses that still surround the Common were constructed. Other than the manor houses, the first substantial house to be built beyond the confines of the High Street was Chester House on Westside, which was built in 1680, reputedly by a merchant called Benjamin Lordell who had made his fortune trading out of Oporto in Portugal. In 1705 the development of Westside continued when another London merchant, William Browne, constructed two substantial houses, Westside House and Warren House (now Cannizaro House). On the south side of the Common, Lingfield House was built in 1715, Lauriston House in 1724, The Grange (formerly known as Wimbledon Villa) in 1747 and Southside House in 1751. It was not until 1759 that formal roads (Westside and Southside) were laid out to cater for the needs of these new householders.

Many of the great houses built in the first half of the 18th century came with substantial estates. The two largest estates were the Wimbledon Park estate which attached to the Duchess's manor house, and the Old Park estate (also known as the Warren estate) which attached to Warren and Westside houses, and which extended back as far as Beverley Brook and Copse Hill. Two other substantial estates attached to Belvedere House (bounded by what are now Church Road, St Mary's Road, Woodside and Wimbledon Hill Road) and Wimbledon House (in the area between Calonne and Lancaster Roads). The final substantial estate in the Wimbledon Village area was the region to the south of Copse Hill. This area had once been arable land but, perhaps due to manpower shortages caused by the bubonic plague, it had been neglected for several centuries, and was known at this time as the Wild Land. The process of taming this land was initiated in 1757 when a successful London goldsmith, Peter Taylor, built an impressive house which he named Prospect Place on the site of what was until recently Atkinson Morley's Hospital. These five substantial estates remained largely intact for over a century, but in due course it was to be their break-up and residential development that shaped Wimbledon Village in the 19th century and beyond.

*4. Sarah Churchill, Duchess of Marlborough, c1691. (Mezzotint by and published by John Smith in 1705, after Sir Godfrey Kneller, © National Portrait Gallery, London)*

# Wimbledon's finest age

There have been peaks and troughs in the rate of the Village's residential development, and the second half of the Georgian era (from the accession of George III in 1760 to the death of George IV in 1830) was something of a trough. Conversely, this was also the period when Wimbledon's role in England's high society and the shaping of the country's political history was at its most prestigious. The Village's finest houses might have been built by bankers and merchants, but in the second half of the 18th century many of them became the residences of some of England's leading statesmen and politicians. These politicians included two future Prime Ministers (the Marquess of Rockingham, who lived on Church Road, and Lord Grenville, who lived in Eagle House) and two of the most radical politicians of the age (John Horne Tooke, who lived in Chester House, and Sir Francis Burdett, who lived in The Grange). Wimbledon's most famous resident statesman was William Wilberforce, who lived at Lauriston House, and who subsequently played a leading role in securing the abolition of the slave trade. With so many politicians living in the area, it is not surprising that William Pitt the Younger (Prime Minister from 1783 to 1801 and again from 1804 to 1806) was a frequent visitor to the Village.

One aspect of development which did feature in this period of the Village's history was the inception of the first significant civic buildings. Prior to the Reformation, local government had been the lord of the manor's responsibility, and was conducted through the Manor Court. This Court convened several times a year, and all of the lord's tenants were required to attend. The power of the Manor Court waned after the Reformation, and responsibility for local government gradually passed to the Vestry. As well as being the room in a church where the clergy changed into their ceremonial vestments, the vestry was also often the room where committees of

27

parishioners would meet to deal with secular matters affecting a church, and the name ultimately attached to this form of local government. Over time the responsibilities of the Vestry grew to encompass wider secular matters within the parish such as maintenance of highways, relief of the poor, and the raising of local rates to finance these activities. During this period the Wimbledon Vestry oversaw the establishment of two buildings designed to help the local poor. These were the Workhouse, built in 1752, and the Free School (an octagonal building, which is now part of The Study school), built shortly after-wards in 1758, both hidden away on Camp Road, a sanitary distance from the centre of the Village.

Another major community project in this period was the rebuilding of St Mary's Church. The previous church, which is thought to have been the second church on the site, had been in existence for more than 500 years, and in addition to being somewhat decrepit it was no longer big enough to accommo-date the Village's growing population. Consequently, a new church was built in 1788. One final community-serving build-ing erected in this period was Wimbledon's iconic windmill. The corn mill was built in 1817 by Charles March, a carpen-ter from Roehampton, "for the advantage and convenience of the neighbourhood".

The influence of the Manor Court may have been waning since the Reformation, but the lord of the manor was still by some way the largest landowner in Wimbledon. In 1744, on the death of the Duchess of Marlborough, the lordship and Marl-borough House passed to her ten-year-old heir, John Spencer, soon to become 1st Earl Spencer. Between 1764 and 1768, Spencer commissioned Capability Brown to landscape the 1,200 acres of Marlborough House, including creating what is now Wimbledon Park Lake. In 1785 Marlborough House was tragically burnt down by a fire which started in the laundry, the maids apparently achieving a rather more comprehensive out-come than their predecessors had managed at Cecil House some 150 years earlier. The second manor house, Belvedere House, was still standing, but had been sold by the Spencer family to a Mrs Martha Rush some years earlier. Consequently, in 1801 the 2nd Earl Spencer elected to build what was to be Wimbledon's fourth and final manor house. This house, which was built close to the ruins of its predecessor, is generally known as Wimbledon Park House, but is sometimes also referred to as Spencer House. The Spencers lived in this house, which was considerably more modest than its predecessor, until 1827. In that year, which marks a convenient end-point to Wimbledon's Georgian history, the Spencer family vacated the house, leasing it to the Duke of Somerset. From that date onwards Wimbledon's lord of the manor was to be an absentee landlord.

*5. Wimbledon Park House, 1826. (Coloured engraving by T.H. Shepherd, published in 1826 by Ackermann, from the collection of The Museum of Wimbledon)*

# Victorian Wimbledon: a railway suburb

At the beginning of the 19th century, Wimbledon remained very much a rural village, and most of the surrounding land was controlled by five large estates (Earl Spencer's Wimbledon Park estate, the Wimbledon House estate off Parkside, the Belvedere estate behind the High Street, the Old Park (or Warren) estate on the west side of the Common, and the Prospect Place estate to the south of Copse Hill). The census of 1801 indicates that Wimbledon had only 1,591 residents, and there were fewer than 20 streets in the Village.

By the time of Queen Victoria's death in 1901 Wimbledon has been transformed into a substantial London suburb. Wimbledon Village had spilled over to create Wimbledon Town, and the population of the enlarged area had grown at the rate of approximately 40% per decade throughout the century (to some 40,000 residents in the census of 1901). By contrast, Wimbledon's population only grew by a further 40% in the entire 20th century.

Wimbledon's rapid population growth in this period reflected a national trend. The underlying cause of this trend was the increased prosperity enjoyed by the country on the back of the Agricultural and Industrial Revolutions. Increased prosperity led to increased birth rates, not least because people could afford to marry earlier. At the same time, factors such as enhanced agricultural productivity, improved sanitation and better health management (for example, the invention of the smallpox vaccine) led to improved mortality rates.

Transport, and in particular the development of the railways, played a key part in Wimbledon's transformation from rural village to London suburb. Wimbledon's first experience of scheduled public transport had been a stage-coach service, known as the Wimbledon Machine, which was introduced in 1780 to run between the Rose & Crown on the High Street and Charing Cross. The coming of the trains, which was ultimately to transform Wimbledon and permit so many of its residents to enjoy the delights of daily commuting, was inaugurated in 1838 with the opening of Wimbledon station. The station was located at the bottom of Wimbledon Hill Road, some way from the Village, to avoid the formidable engineering challenge of having to propel trains up the hill. The arrival of the trains did not precipitate the overnight expansion of Wimbledon Town. It was to be another 20 years or so before development of the Town really took off. By that time Wimbledon station had become an increasingly important hub, serving a number of onward destinations. Perhaps more significantly, Wimbledon Town benefited in the 1850s from the introduction into the area of new water mains.

During the remainder of the 19th century two further stations were to open in the vicinity of the Village which would have an influence of the rate of development within the area. In 1871 Raynes Park station was opened, and this precipitated development in the area south of Copse Hill. In 1889 Wimbledon Park tube station opened and the District Line was extended to Wimbledon, encouraging further development in the Wimbledon Park area.

The availability of land in the Village area was of course not infinite, and the demand for increased housing was only met because the owners of Wimbledon's five large estates were ultimately prepared to see their estates sold off and broken up for development. The first estate to be broken up was the largest of them all, Earl Spencer's Wimbledon Park estate. Having previously vacated the manor house in 1827, letting it to the Duke of Somerset, in 1846 the 4th Earl Spencer sold the manor house and the surrounding estate to a London businessman and property developer, John Augustus Beaumont. Beaumont went about developing the northern half of the estate in the 1850s, and then moved on to the southern half in the 1870s. In 1872, during this second development phase, he sold Wimbledon Park House itself to a Mrs Evans, who was to be the first of a succession of relatively short-term owners over the next 75 years.

The second estate to be sold off for development was the Prospect Place estate at the other end of the Village. In 1831 Prospect Place had been purchased by Charles Pepys, subsequently Earl of Cottenham, who was to become Queen Victoria's first Lord Chancellor. On Pepys's death in 1851 his family sold Prospect Place to the Duke of Wellington and the surrounding estate to developers. These developers laid out a number of streets in the region of Cottenham Park Road, although the residential development of the area only really took off after the opening of Raynes Park station in 1871.

The break-up and development of the remaining three estates did not occur until the start of the 20th century. One

*6. Prospect Place House, c1770. (Photograph by G.C. Druce of an engraving by J. Roberts of a painting by an unknown artist, from the collection of The Museum of Wimbledon)*

other area where development did begin in the 19th century was the land between the Common and the Ridgway which attached to the large houses on Southside Common (hereafter Southside). The first street to be laid out here was Lingfield Road in the 1850s, and by 1907 all five of the interconnecting streets that exist today had been established.

As well as residential development, the Victorian era witnessed the construction of many buildings designed to service the Village's burgeoning population. The first major new building to go up in the post-Georgian era was the present St Mary's Church. The previous church had only been built 55 years earlier, but it was already too small for the community, and so in 1843 Sir George Gilbert Scott was commissioned to build a bigger church. Even this new church, the fourth and final church to be built on this site, proved to be insufficient for the Village's expanding population, and in 1859 a second church, Christ Church, was constructed at the top of Copse Hill. The final church to go up in the Village during this era was Emmanuel Church on the Ridgway, which was founded in 1888 by a breakaway group of some of the more evangelical members of the St Mary's congregation. The number of new churches catering for the spiritual needs of the community was at least matched by the number of new pubs catering for their more secular needs. Of the pubs which remain today, the Fox & Grapes is first mentioned in1832 (under its original name, the Union Beershop), The Swan in 1855 and the Hand in Hand in 1867.

Shortly after the last of these three pubs opened for business the Village acquired its first hospital. This was the Wimbledon Cottage Hospital, opened in 1870 on Thurstan Road, and funded initially by local subscriptions. This hospital continued to serve the Village until its closure in 1983. In 1869, one year before the opening of the hospital, Atkinson Morley's Convalescent Hospital had opened on Copse Hill to provide a facility for the recovering patients of St George's Hospital, which at

33

that time was located not in Tooting but on Hyde Park Corner. The convalescent hospital was funded by a legacy from a Mr Atkinson Morley, a wealthy hotelier who had once been a medical student at St George's, and was built in the grounds of the recently demolished Prospect Place.

The Victorian era also witnessed the foundation of several schools which remain in operation. Rokeby School (originally known as Helmsley School and now relocated to Kingston upon Thames) opened on Woodhayes Road in 1877, The Study School was launched on the High Street in 1893, and King's College School ('KCS') relocated from The Strand in London to its existing site on Southside in 1897. Two final new establishments from this time that merit a mention are the Village Club, which opened on the Ridgway in 1859, and Wimbledon's public library, which opened on Wimbledon Hill Road in 1887.

As Wimbledon's population multiplied in the 19th century, so the demands on local government also grew, and gradually began to outstrip the capacity of the Vestry, which had been looking after the Village's affairs since the Reformation. In 1866 a new administrative body, known as the Local Board of Health, was set up in the Village. The Local Board, which consisted of 15 members elected by ratepayers, initially had responsibility for health-related matters such as sanitation. Over time its role gradually increased to take on almost all of the Vestry's responsibilities, and in 1885 that body was disbanded. In 1878, in a move which symbolised the growing importance of the Town relative to the Village, the Local Board relocated to offices on the Broadway which subsequently became Wimbledon's first town hall. Whilst the Vestry had governed for some 300 years, Wimbledon's local government needs outgrew the capacity of the Local Board within 30 years, and in 1895 it was upgraded, expanded and transformed into an Urban District Council. Wimbledon's new substance as a significant London suburb had been further acknowledged in

1885 when, under the Redistribution of Seats Act, it had became a parliamentary constituency with its own MP.

Although Wimbledon Village's role in London's high society may have peaked in Georgian era, one annual event in particular ensured that it continued to play a part on London's social scene in the Victorian age. This event was the annual meeting on the Common of the National Rifle Association ('NRA'). The NRA had been founded in 1859 by the 5th Earl Spencer, in conjunction with the Duke of Cambridge, to hone the skills of Britain's soldiers in the face of the perceived threat of French invasion. For one week every summer between 1860 and 1889, the area of the Common by the Windmill became a tented village for the annual NRA meeting, and large crowds

*7. National Rifle Association Meeting, 1864. (Coloured illustration entitled 'The Rifle Contest, Wimbledon', published in The Illustrated London News, from the collection of The Museum of Wimbledon)*

would descend on the Village to enjoy the spectacle. Queen Victoria fired the first shot at the opening meeting, and awarded a prize of £250 to the best marksman. The event flourished, but by 1889 it had grown too large for its temporary premises in a semi-residential area, and the NRA relocated to the permanent premises at Bisley which it still occupies. Two years later the Common was to host another military event attracting London's elite. In 1891 the Common was the setting for a review of troops put on for the benefit of Kaiser Wilhelm II, who was both Emperor of Germany and Queen Victoria's grandson, and who 23 years later was to become the principal object of British loathing during the First World War.

This is primarily a history of the development that has taken place in Wimbledon Village over the ages, but equally as important to the character of the Village today have been some of the developments that have been successfully resisted. In particular, we owe the preservation of the Common to such opposition. In 1864, the 5th Earl Spencer introduced a Bill to the House of Lords proposing to develop Putney Heath and to enclose and improve Wimbledon Common, which the Earl maintained was swamp-ridden, rubbish-strewn and overrun by Gypsies. The Earl's plans provoked vociferous local opposition, led by several of Wimbledon's principal landowners, in particular Sir Henry Peek, MP, who formed a Wimbledon Commons Committee to fight the proposals. After a prolonged struggle the Earl was defeated and, in 1871 under the Wimbledon and Putney Commons Act, the Earl's rights to the Common were passed in perpetuity to a body of Conservators in return for an annual rent of £1,200. The Conservators were tasked with preserving the Common "for public and local use for the purpose of exercise and recreation". They had their first success in preserving the Common just four years later when they succeeded in blocking John Sawbridge-Erle-Drax's plans to develop Caesar's Camp. Their responsibility for the Common remains in place to this day.

# The 20th century and beyond

Having surged throughout the 19th century, the rate of population growth in Wimbledon as a whole slowed down substantially in the 20th century. The same was not true of the rate of residential development in the Village. In the last 50 years of the 19th century, there had been an average of six new streets developed in the Village each decade. In the 20th century, the average rate of development was closer to 11 streets per decade, apart from the entire two decades dominated by the two World Wars when only one new street was completed (Preston Road). In the first half of the 20th century, the main facilitator of new development was the break-up of the three remaining large estates in the Village area.

The development of two of these three estates began almost simultaneously in 1900. That year witnessed the demolition of both Belvedere House, which had been Wimbledon's second manor house, and Wimbledon House on Parkside. Belvedere House had been purchased in 1834 by a Lambeth timber merchant, James Courthope Peache, and the estate had remained in his family until his grandson, also James Courthope Peache, sold it to the Belvedere Estate Company for development. Wimbledon House was by all accounts an undistinguished building, but it had had a succession of distinguished owners, culminating in Sir Henry Peek, MP. On Peek's death, his son sold the estate to the Wimbledon House Estate Company for development. The developers acknowledged the heritage of Wimbledon House by naming several of the streets which they laid out on the estate after some of its more famous residents (Calonne Road, Marryat Road and Peek Crescent).

The third and final estate to be developed was the Old Park estate, which ran north of Copse Hill from Westside all the way down to Beverley Brook. The estate, which included both Westside and Warren (subsequently Cannizaro) Houses, had passed by marriage to the Drax family in 1827. We have already encountered one of the Drax family, John Sawbridge-Erle-Drax, in connection with the desecration of Caesar's Camp. The break-up of the Old Park estate was the responsibility of one of his successors, the even more splendidly named Admiral the Honourable Sir Reginald Aylmer Ranfurly Plunkett-Ernle-Erle-Drax. The development of the Old Park estate began in 1924, and concluded shortly after the outbreak of the Second World War with the completion of Preston Road. Several of the roads on the estate were named after the Drax family's extensive landholdings in Dorset, and a couple were named after ships with which the Admiral had been associated.

In physical terms, Wimbledon Village survived the First World War completely unscathed. Like most other communities in the country Wimbledon did suffer great human loss, and in 1921 a war memorial was erected on the edge of the Common to commemorate the 200 or so Wimbledon men who had lost their lives at war.

The physical damage suffered by the Village was much greater in the Second World War. Like the rest of London, Wimbledon had to endure the brutal pummelling of the Blitz in 1940 and 1941, and the more insidious attacks of V-1 rockets in 1944. The story of Wimbledon at war is meticulously described in Norman Plastow's book 'Safe as Houses'. In total, some 150 Wimbledon residents lost their lives to German bombs, and a further 440 were seriously injured. Unfortunately, not all houses were safe, and over 800 of them were either destroyed or damaged beyond repair.

After the euphoria of victory, Britain had to endure several further years of belt-tightening austerity as society and the economy slowly recovered from the ravages of war. In Wimbledon Village, this meant that no further new roads were developed in the remainder of the 1940s. In the 1950s, by contrast, Wimbledon witnessed a major recovery in the rate of new building. Many of the new streets were built on the grounds of large Victorian houses which had been irreparably damaged during the war, and which had to be demolished. Other streets were built to rehouse those who had lost their homes in the war. A new council estate, for example, was built off Westside on the land behind Chester House. Other new streets are best described as in-fills, occupying spare land between existing residential developments. The surge in building activity lasted until approximately 1990. Since then the rate of expansion has slowed substantially, at least for now. In period since the turn of the 21st century there have been only three new streets laid out in the Village (Atkinson Close, Cedar Park Gardens and Rydon Mews).

Although the spread of new housing continued apace in the second half of the century, it was not completely unfettered. The spirit of opposition to developments that would have sacrificed the Village's green spaces continued to halt the worst excesses of prospective developers throughout the century. The first such campaign kicked off in 1902 when the Wimbledon House Estate Company announced plans to build a block of flats on The Green. These plans met with stern opposition, and the Company's directors were eventually forced to abandon their plans for flats, settling instead for three houses. In 1903 the men who had opposed this development, led by Pall Mall Gazette journalist Richardson Evans, formed a local conservation society, which he christened the John Evelyn Club in honour of the 17th-century diarist whom he regarded as the patron saint of conservation. This club, which changed its name to the Wimbledon Society in 1982, has continued to fight conservation battles for over a century, and can take a large amount of credit for the successful conservation of much that we value in and around the Village of today. One such success came in 1938 when the Drax family were threatening to develop land on the Old Park estate which they had previously let to the Royal Wimbledon Golf Club, and the John Evelyn Club succeeded in persuading the Council to buy the land and extend the golf club's lease. One of the Club's other achieve-

*8. The Village Club & Lecture Hall, 1925 (Photograph by H.C. Archer, from the collection of The Museum of Wimbledon)*

ments was the creation, in 1916, of a Museum of Wimbledon on the top floor of the Village Club on the Ridgway. The Museum, like the Society itself, continues to thrive and is well worth a visit.

Another major conservation victory secured the survival of Wimbledon Park. In 1886 John Augustus Beaumont had died, leaving what remained of his Wimbledon Park estate to his daughter, Augusta Beaumont. Augusta, who had no sentimental interest in Wimbledon Park, drew up aggressive plans for the Park's further development, including draining Capability Brown's lake and, at a later date, running roads across the Park to the edge of the new District Line. Amid increasing local anxiety at these plans the Council eventually intervened in 1914 and secured parliamentary consent to buy what remained of Wimbledon Park to preserve it for the community.

The need for citizens to remain vigilant to protect the

environment that we value remains as important today as ever. One recent conservation success has been the campaign fought in the last decade by 'LUNG' ('Land for Urban Neighbourhood Greenspace'), to preserve for the community the green space now named Morley Park on part of the Copse Hill site previously occupied by the Atkinson Morley's Hospital.

The local governance of Wimbledon underwent further change in the 20th century. In terms of Wimbledon's self-esteem, there was a high point and a low point. The high point came in 1905 on Charter Day when, with royal assent, Wimbledon was formally granted borough status, and with it the entitlement to elect a mayor. The low point came 60 years later when, in 1965, a review of local government efficiency concluded that Wimbledon should be transferred from the county of Surrey into the new county of Greater London, where it was to form part of 'Borough Number 22' in conjunction with Merton, Morden and Mitcham. The final indignity came when Wimbledon lost out to Merton in a scrap to secure naming rights to the new borough.

On the subject of local governance, the last decades of the 20th century witnessed the final demise of the remaining vestiges of influence wielded by Wimbledon's original local authority, the lord of the manor. In 1949 Wimbledon Park House, the last in the line of the four manor houses to be built in Wimbledon, was finally demolished. In 1968 the 8th Earl Spencer, Princess Diana's father, accepted a lump sum in full and final settlement of the annual rent payable to him by the Wimbledon Common Conservators. Finally, in 1996 the 9th Earl Spencer, Princess Diana's brother, sold the title to the Lordship of the Manor of Wimbledon (a title which by now carried no financial rights) to a mystery bidder based in South America for the impressive sum of £171,000.

Within Wimbledon as a whole, the 20th century witnessed a continuing shift of civic emphasis away from the Village in favour of the Town. This trend started at the very beginning of the century when, in 1900, there was a disastrous fire at Cannizaro House which the fire brigade, then resident at a new fire station on the High Street in the Village, failed to extinguish because their hoses would not reach from Rushmere Pond on the Common. The Council's response was to relocate the fire station to new premises on Queens Road in the Town. Another symptom, later in the century, was the closure of the Village's two NHS hospitals, Wimbledon Hospital on Thurstan Road (closed in 1983) and Atkinson Morley's nearby on Copse Hill (closed in 2003). It is perhaps indicative of the Village's latter-day status that the year in which Wimbledon Hospital was closed was also the year in which a substantial private hospital, Parkside, was opened.

Wimbledon Village may no longer be a locus of civic authority, but the social status that it first acquired in the 18th century, and which it retained in the 19th century courtesy of

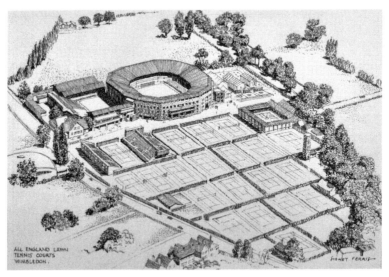

*9. All England Lawn Tennis & Croquet Club, 1960. (Pen & Indian ink drawing by Sidney G. Ferris, from the collection of The Museum of Wimbledon)*

the National Rifle Association, survives very much intact on the back of its reputation as the venue for the world's most famous tennis championship. The Club that we know today as the All England Lawn Tennis & Croquet Club was founded as a croquet club in 1868 in a field off Worple Road, just outside the Village. The craze-like popularity of croquet proved to be short-lived, but the club's founders had the foresight to convert their lawns to accommodate the emerging new game of tennis, and in 1877 the club held the first open tennis championship. The championship rapidly became a popular event on the London social calendar, and by 1922 the Worple Road premises had become too small, prompting the club to purchase from the Beaumont estate the grounds in Church Road which it continues to occupy. Since then the Wimbledon Tennis Championship has gone from strength to strength, and ensures that, for two weeks each summer, Wimbledon Village sits firmly at the centre of the world's sporting and social stage.

# THE STREETS OF
# WIMBLEDON VILLAGE

## 1. Alan Road

Alan Road was laid out in 1905 in the grounds of what had been Belvedere House. This house was the second of four manor houses to be built in Wimbledon between 1588 and 1801. It was built in 1720 by a wealthy Huguenot City merchant, Sir Theodore Janssen. Sir Theodore had purchased Wimbledon's original manor house (Cecil House) three years earlier for £27,000, but had rapidly concluded that it was in such a state of disrepair that it had to be demolished and a new one built. Sadly, Sir Theodore did not enjoy his new manor house for long. Shortly after its completion he lost his fortune on the collapse of the South Sea Company, and was forced to sell the manor house and retire to a considerably smaller house on nearby Church Road.

After several further owners, the second manor house was eventually purchased in 1834 by James Courthope Peache, a Lambeth timber merchant. It was James who christened the house Belvedere House. The house passed from James Courthope Peache to his children, Alfred and Kezia Peache, and then to his grandson, also James Courthope Peache. In 1900, this latter James Courthope Peache sold the estate to the Belvedere Estate Company, and the development of the surrounding roads, including Alan Road, began the following year.

Alan Road is one of three roads in the Village named after individuals where the reason behind the name is somewhat speculative. The name Alan first appears in the Peache family tree in 1892 when one of James Courthope Peache's sons is named Henry Alan Peache. Given that there are no ancestors named Alan, it is possible that he was given this name to commemorate a close family friend or business associate whose name was also remembered when Alan Road was laid out some years later. Unfortunately, no records exist to confirm precisely why the Peache family chose to give Alan Road its name.

## 2. Alfreton Close

Hot on the heels of Alan Road, Alfreton Close is one of only two Village streets the name of which is a complete mystery, albeit a relatively recent one. Alfreton Close was only laid out in 1971, but there appears to be no record of the reason for its name. The name was probably proposed by the street's developer. It is possible that it was named after the town of Alfreton in Derbyshire, but there is no known link with Wimbledon.

Alfreton Close was built off Parkside on the site of a large house called Wressil Lodge which had been home to an eminent Victorian colonial administrator, Sir Henry Bartle Edward Frere. Sir Henry had a glittering career in India, rising to become Governor of Bombay, before being made High Commissioner for Southern Africa in 1877. In Africa, the glitter on Sir Henry's career was tarnished when his efforts to impose a British confederation on the region contributed substantially to the Zulu and Boer wars. Sir Henry was recalled to London to face charges of misconduct, and spent his final years in Wressil Lodge on Parkside prior to his death in 1884.

Sir Henry is commemorated by streets in Karachi, Durban and Johannesburg. There is an entire suburb named for him in Mombasa (Freretown) and a mountain in Queensland, Australia. It is perhaps a shame that Alfreton Close was not named either Wressil Close after the house which it supplanted or Frere Close after its most famous resident.

*10. Sir Henry Bartle Edward Frere, c1870. (Photograph by an unknown photographer, © National Portrait Gallery, London)*

## 3. Allington Close

In the 19th century, this close, which runs off the High Street, was densely populated with overcrowded tenement buildings. It enjoyed a variety of names over the years before it finally became known as Allington Close.

At one stage it was known as Dog & Fox Court after the nearby pub. In the rate books of 1838 it is referred to rather less glamorously as Mutton Alley. By the time of the 1861 census it had again taken the name of an adjacent pub, and was known as Beehive Place. It was eventually christened Allington Close in 1937 after Allington Lodge, Merton Park, which was home to the landlord of the tenements.

## 4. Almer Road

The residential development of Wimbledon Village has been based upon the development of five great estates. We have already encountered one of these in Belvedere House. The last estate to be sold off for development was the Old Park, which was owned by the Drax family. The Old Park (also known as Warren Park) extended from Westside all the way to Beverley Brook. The Drax family acquired the estate by marriage in 1827.

In 1924 the head of the Drax family was the elaborately named Admiral the Honourable Sir Reginald Aylmer Ranfurly Plunkett-Ernle-Erle-Drax (hereafter Admiral Drax), of whom more later. He began the process of selling off his estate in that year, and over the next 15 years the following roads were developed and given names linked to the Admiral and his family: Almer Road, Barham Road, Drax Avenue, Dunstall Road, Ellerton Road, Ernle Road, Hood Road, McKay Road, Preston Road and Wool Road.

Although they owned a large chunk of Wimbledon, the main family seat of the Drax family was, and still is, Charborough

House in Dorset. Almer Road is named after the Dorset village of Almer which is adjacent to the Drax estate. The village name derives from the Old English 'ael mere', meaning eel pond, and refers to a small pool on the River Winterborne south-east of the village.

## 5. Arthur Road

Arthur Road was built on the estate of Wimbledon Park House (sometimes known as Spencer House). This house was the fourth and final manor house to be built in Wimbledon. It was built in 1801 by George, 2nd Earl Spencer, after the third manor house (known as Marlborough House because it had been commissioned by George's ancestor Sarah Churchill, Duchess of Marlborough), had burnt to the ground in 1785.

The Spencers lived in Wimbledon Park House until 1827, in which year they let the house to the Duke of Somerset. Subsequently, in 1846 they sold the house and surrounding estate (with the Duke of Somerset still in residence) to John Augustus Beaumont.

Beaumont's wealth came from his family's interests in the County Fire Insurance Company, a company founded by his father and of which Beaumont was now managing director. Surprisingly, given the impact that he was to have on the development of Wimbledon, very little is known about Beaumont. We do know that he had one big adventure in his youth which may have accounted for the entrepreneurial flair which he demonstrated in later life. In 1824 Beaumont's father, Barber Beaumont, had entered into a collaboration with the Argentinian authorities to develop a settlement in Argentina to be populated by independent farmers transported from the UK. The project got into difficulties shortly after its inception when war broke out between Argentina and Brazil and the Argentinian authorities defaulted on their commitments. In 1826 Barber Beaumont despatched his son, John Augustus

Beaumont, to South America to try to salvage the project. Beaumont's mission was meant to last for a few weeks but ended up taking 17 months. Ultimately, he was unsuccessful in his task, but not before he had experienced many adventures, including meetings with the Argentinian president, a mutiny on his ship which he was forced to quell at gunpoint, a period of imprisonment over a disputed passport and several hazardous treks through the Argentinian outback.

Beaumont had bought the Wimbledon Park House estate to develop it. Chronologically, it was the first of the five large estates in Wimbledon to be broken up. Beaumont developed the estate in two phases, and the second phase, which commenced in 1872, included Leopold Road, Home Park Road, Lake Road and Arthur Road. Arthur Road was patriotically named after Queen Victoria's third son, Arthur, Duke of Connaught. It is reputed that Beaumont's son-in-law, Colonel

*11. Arthur Road, c1913. (Photograph by Richardson Evans, from the collection of The Museum of Wimbledon)*

49

Lane, had saved Prince Arthur's life when they had served together in the army in India.

Arthur Road was not named after the legendary King Arthur, notwithstanding that nearby streets have subsequently been named Lancelot Court and Camelot Close.

## 6. Atherton Drive

Atherton Drive was laid out in 1935 on the site of a house called Atherton Grange, after which the road was named. Atherton Grange had been built somewhere between 1850 and 1869 on land sold off by John Augustus Beaumont.

Atherton Grange had had a variety of distinguished and slightly less distinguished residents in the second half of the 19th century. Falling into the latter category was THV Lukey, who was resident in 1869, and who was a celebrated breeder of mastiff dogs. MB Wynn, author of 'A History of Mastiffs', recalls visiting Atherton Grange and THV Lukey "proposing a short walk across the Common, taking his dogs with him; he insisted on our calling at a posting house and, much to my horror, ordered a gallon of beer. I asked him numerous questions about the pedigree of his dogs, but found he was somewhat confused".

Soon afterwards, in 1879, the house was purchased by John Dillwyn Llewelyn, a pioneering early photographer. In 1856 the Illustrated London News had celebrated him "as a gentleman to whom all photographers owe a world of thanks".

By 1897 the house had changed hands again and was owned by Heywood Walter Seton-Karr, a celebrated soldier, adventurer, hunter and amateur archaeologist. He brought back collections of ancient flints from several of his expeditions which represented the first evidence of Stone Age man in tropical Africa and, in the opinion of others at the time, demonstrated the unity of Palaeolithic races in Asia, Europe and Africa. Seton-Karr's interest in archaeology was not exclusively academic. In 1897 he wrote to General Pitt Rivers, founder of the eponymous archaeology and anthropology museum in Oxford, "I think there are over 2,000 Somaliland palaeo, and I had better say at once that I want (1) £200 for 100 specimens which may be selected by yourself, or (2) £400 for the lot".

## 7. Atkinson Close

At the time of writing Atkinson Close is the newest street in the Village, having been laid out in 2014 on the site of the former Atkinson Morley's Hospital. The hospital was named after its eponymous benefactor, Atkinson Morley, who had been a medical student at St George's Hospital in the first half of the 19th century when that hospital was located on Hyde Park Corner. Morley subsequently abandoned medicine, and went on to have a prosperous career as an hotelier, becoming proprietor of two leading London hotels, the Burlington on Cork Street and the Morley on Trafalgar Square. Morley became a governor of St George's Hospital, and on his death in 1858 he bequeathed £150,000 to the Hospital to build a home outside of London "for receiving, maintaining and generally assisting convalescent poor patients".

The legacy was received just as one of Wimbledon's five large estates, Prospect Place on Copse Hill, was about to become the second estate to be broken up for development. The doctors of St George's were, initially, uncertain about the suitability of the site, expressing concerns that "the proximity to London rendered the locality liable during the prevalence of the east wind to have the air tainted with the smoke of the metropolis, and possible with a south or west wind the damp rising from the valley would be objectionable". They eventually relented, and St George's purchased 28 acres of the estate to construct Atkinson Morley's Convalescent Hospital, which opened in 1869.

Convalescence remained the purpose of the hospital until the start of the Second World War, when the hospital was converted to a neurosurgical unit. This remained its function until 2003 when these services were transferred to the main St George's Hospital, which by this time had relocated to Tooting, and Atkinson Morley's was closed.

After extensive delays and planning disputes, the former hospital grounds and buildings are being converted into residential housing to be named Wimbledon Hill Park. This seems a slightly oblique choice of name given that the development is close to neither Wimbledon Hill Road nor Wimbledon Park.

## 8. Barham Road

Barham Road, which was laid out in 1929, was another road developed by Admiral Drax on the Old Park estate. This road follows the route of what was originally a drive leading to Warren Farm on the Common.

Barham Road was named by Admiral Drax after HMS Barham, the ship which he was commanding in 1929. HMS Barham was built in 1914 and served in both World Wars. In 1941, while on active service in the Mediterranean, she was hit and sunk by a German submarine off the coast of Egypt with the loss of over 800 men. She was one of only two British battleships, alongside HMS Royal Oak, to be sunk by a German submarine in the Second World War.

HMS Barham had itself been named after Admiral Charles Middleton, 1st Baron Barham. Middleton was a naval officer and politician who rose to become First Lord of the Admiralty in 1805. There is a link between Middleton and one of Wimbledon's most famous former residents, William Wilberforce. Middleton, prompted by his Christian faith, became a strong supporter of the movement to abolish the slave trade, and was instrumental in persuading William Wilberforce to take up this cause in Parliament.

## 9. Bathgate Road

Bathgate Road, which was laid out in 1873, was another road developed by John Augustus Beaumont on the Wimbledon Park House estate. The street was initially known as New Park Road because Wimbledon Park had originally been known as New Park to distinguish it from the Old Park on the other side of Wimbledon Common.

New Park Road was renamed Bathgate Road in 1911 after Alderman Bathgate, three times mayor of Wimbledon. John Marshall Bathgate was a Scot who had started his working career in the Clydesdale Steel Works, but subsequently moved to London and rose through the ranks to become a director of Pearsons, the publishing company. In addition to serving three times as Wimbledon's mayor he was an enthusiastic member of the local Conservative party, and a justice of the peace. He died in 1953.

If John Augustus Beaumont's daughter, Augusta, had had her way, Bathgate Road would have been considerably longer than it is today. Augusta inherited the Wimbledon Park House estate on her father's death in 1886, and started to make plans to develop the whole of Wimbledon Park, including draining the lake. At one stage these plans included extending Bathgate Road to run all the way across the park to meet the new underground line. It was these plans that prompted the Wimbledon Council to acquire what was left of Wimbledon Park in 1914 to protect it from future development.

## 10. Beech Close

Beech Close was developed as a council estate in 1955 during the housing boom that followed the post-war austerity years. This was a time of renewed optimism, and several of the streets laid out in this decade have poetically descriptive names rather unsubtly designed to help estate agents lure new residents to

Wimbledon's leafy domain. Beech Close is one such street, although in fairness the name is entirely justified because the close, which backs onto Cannizaro Park, does benefit from more than its fair share of mature trees, many of them beeches.

## 11. Beltane Drive

Beltane Drive was laid out in 1959 and was named after the school of that name which occupied what is now Queensmere House in Royal Close. Beltane had been founded in the 1930s by two teachers, Andrew and Joan Tomlinson, and at the time was regarded as highly progressive, "relaxed, co-educational and international". Many of the pupils were Jewish children whose families had fled from Europe. One such pupil was the distinguished Hungarian mathematician, Raoul Bott. He wrote of his time at Beltane that "in one stroke it made me into a life-time Anglophile as well as a great admirer of the opposite sex".

Beltane is the Celtic name for the May Day. Andrew Tomlinson explained that he and his wife picked this name because when they acquired the building their objective was to be up and running by the following 1st May. The Tomlinsons had distinctly left wing political leanings, and many pupils believed that it was no coincidence that the school was named after what was also International Workers' Day. In 1936, Beltane co-hosted a garden party for the Society for Cultural Relations with the USSR which was attended by the Russian ambassador.

When war broke out the Tomlinsons moved Beltane to a country house in Wiltshire. The school eventually closed down in 1952 when the Tomlinsons moved to Italy. Beltane Drive is one of two streets in the Village named after a school, the other being Rokeby Place.

## 12–15. Belvedere Avenue, Drive, Grove & Square

These roads are named after Belvedere House, the second great manor house in Wimbledon already encountered under Alan Road. Belvedere House was purchased and named in 1834 by Lambeth timber merchant James Courthope Peache. Peache chose the name Belvedere House after the street in which he had lived and on which he had his business in Lambeth. Belvedere Road still exists today, running behind Jubilee Gardens and the London Eye.

A belvedere, which takes its name from the Italian for beautiful view, is an architectural structure, often a pavilion or tower on the top of a building, located to take advantage of a scenic view.

Belvedere House was demolished in 1900 to make way for

*12. Belvedere House, date unknown. (Photograph by Mrs Woodward of an earlier picture by an unknown artist, from the collection of The Museum of Wimbledon)*

the development of the surrounding estate, and Belvedere Avenue, Drive and Grove were laid out between 1900 and 1907.

Belvedere Square has a slightly older provenance, having been built in 1864 by Peache's children, Alfred and Kezia, as cottages for workers on the Belvedere estate. This area had previously been a builder's yard on the estate. The road was originally known as Belvedere Cottages, and was renamed Belvedere Square in 1930.

## 16. Beverley Avenue

Beverley Avenue was laid out in 1935, and was named after nearby Beverley Brook. This brook, which rises in Worcester Park and flows for some nine miles before entering the Thames at Barn Elms, has one of the most ancient names in Wimbledon. Beverley Brook is first recorded by name as Beferithi in 693AD (in an 11th century copy of an Anglo-Saxon charter). In 1548 it was recorded as Beverey, and in 1822 as Baveley Brook. The name comes from the Old English beofor rithig, meaning 'small stream frequented by beavers'.

Beavers were a native British animal, but were hunted for their meat, pelts and scent glands until they became extinct in England by the 12th century and in Scotland by the 16th century. There are currently pilot schemes underway in Devon and Scotland to explore the feasibility of re-introducing beavers to the UK.

In the Middle Ages, Beverley Brook must have been a rather larger stream than it is today, because in addition to beavers it used to support a watermill at Beverley Meads close to the bottom of Wimbledon Common.

## 17. Burdett Avenue

Burdett Avenue was laid out in 1933, and is named after Sir Francis Burdett, MP, who lived in Wimbledon Villa (subsequently The Grange) on Southside from 1801 to 1812.

Sir Francis was a radical politician who objected to both major parties and who dedicated his political career to campaigning for parliamentary reform. He was a great friend and disciple of another leading radical politician of the time, John Horne Tooke, who lived across the Common at Chester House on Westside.

Sir Francis was twice imprisoned for his political convictions, once in the Tower of London. He was first imprisoned in 1810 for an alleged breach of parliamentary privilege, and again in 1820 for his outspoken criticism of the Peterloo Massacre in Manchester (when the authorities had permitted the cavalry to charge a crowd demonstrating for parliamentary reform, killing at least a dozen demonstrators and wounding a great many more). He is best known in Wimbledon for having fought a duel on the Common in 1807 against another politician, John Paull. Both men were injured but survived, and on this occasion Sir Francis does not appear to have been imprisoned.

Sir Francis died in 1844, grief-stricken and having refused to eat following the death of his wife ten days earlier.

## 18. Burghley Road

Burghley Road was laid out in 1901, shortly after the sale for development of the Wimbledon House estate (see following entry for Calonne Road). Burghley Road is named after the Burghleys, who have as good a claim as any to be Wimbledon's founding family. Sir William Cecil, 1st Lord Burghley, was an English statesman and chief counsellor to Elizabeth I for most of her reign. He served two terms as her Secretary

*13. Sir Francis Burdett, 1810. (Line engraving by William Sharp, after James Northcote, published in 1811, © National Portrait Gallery, London)*

of State (1550–1553 and 1558–1572) and was Lord High Treasurer from 1572. In 1550 Sir William acquired the Old Rectory in Wimbledon as a grace and favour home. The history of the Old Rectory, which still stands to the north of St Mary's Church, is described later in this book under Rectory Orchard. Suffice to say here that it is Wimbledon's oldest surviving house, having been built in 1500. Sir William lived in the Old Rectory until 1564 when he passed the lease to a friend, William Bowyer.

It was Sir William's son, Sir Thomas Cecil, Earl of Exeter and subsequently 2nd Lord Burghley, who really put Wimbledon on the map. In 1576 Sir Thomas, who had lived in the Old Rectory as a child, purchased the lordship of the manor of Wimbledon. Until 1536 this lordship had been held, as an offshoot of the manor of Mortlake, by successive Archbishops of Canterbury. In that year the Archbishop had been forced to hand over the manorship to Henry VIII during the seizure by the Crown of Church property that accompanied the dissolution of the monasteries and the Reformation. The manorship had a succession of owners in the following few years, including Henry VIII's chief minister Thomas Cromwell and his last wife, Catherine Parr, before it was acquired by Sir Thomas.

By all accounts Sir Thomas did not share his father's political acumen. Indeed, his father is reputed to have said that Sir Thomas was not fit to govern a tennis court. Nevertheless, Sir Thomas left a greater mark on Wimbledon's local history than his father, because it was he who built Wimbledon's first great manor house. Cecil House, as it became known, was located close to what is today Home Park Road, and was completed in 1588, the year of the Spanish Armada. It was by far the largest of the four manor houses which were to be built in Wimbledon over the subsequent centuries, and was the closest that Wimbledon has ever come to having its own palace.

*14. Burghley Road, c1929. (Postcard published by J. Salmon of Sevenoaks, from the author's collection)*

## 19. Calonne Road

Calonne Road was laid out in 1900 in the grounds of what had been Wimbledon House. This house probably ranks as the most significant house in the history of the Village after the four Wimbledon manor houses and the Old Rectory. It was built in approximately 1710 on Parkside, close to where Marryat Road is today. Its first owner was Sir Theodore Janssen, who went on to acquire the lordship of Wimbledon and the Cecil manor house in 1717, and who demolished Cecil House in order to build Belvedere House, Wimbledon's second manor house.

Wimbledon House stood for 190 years before it was demolished in 1900 by the Wimbledon House Estate Company, set up to develop the surrounding estate. Mr Hampton, the estate agent who won the lucrative contract to sell off plots on the estate (and whose eponymous estate agency still sits on the corner of the High Street and Marryat Road) wrote that "if ever there was an old and historical mansion that deserved its demolition it was Wimbledon House". Of course, he did have a fairly large vested interest in its demise.

Wimbledon House had had an array of famous residents, and to the credit of the Wimbledon House Estate Company the roads which they developed on the estate were named after several of them. These included Joseph and Charlotte Marryat (Marryat Place and Road), Sir Henry Peek (Peek Crescent) and Charles Alexandre, Vicomte de Calonne. Other well-known residents whom they might also have commemorated had included John 'Vulture' Hopkins, a wealthy banker who acquired extensive property in the Village along Southside, Ridgway and Worple Road, and Louis Joseph de Bourbon, Prince of Conde, a French noble who had fled France in 1789 after the fall of the Bastille to escape the guillotine.

Charles Alexandre, Vicomte de Calonne, was another emi-

*15. Wimbledon House, 1826. (Coloured engraving by T.H. Shepherd, published in 1826 by Ackermann, from the collection of The Museum of Wimbledon)*

61

ent Frenchman who had fled the Revolution. In 1783 Calonne had been appointed Controller-General of Finances in France (the equivalent of our Chancellor of the Exchequer). In this capacity he had tried to implement a radical programme of tax reform. His plans had met with strong opposition, and he was dismissed from office in 1787. Calonne left France shortly afterwards, came to England and purchased Wimbledon House in 1791. The Victorian historian Thomas Carlyle was perhaps a little uncharitable to Wimbledon when he wrote of Calonne that "a tempest of public opinion blew him out of France into outer darkness". Calonne was finally granted permission by Napoleon Bonaparte to return to France in 1802, but he died about a month after his return.

Today Calonne Road is home to perhaps the most exotic building to have been constructed in the Village since the Second World War, the Buddhapadipa Temple, the first Buddhist temple to have been built in the United Kingdom. Originally established in Richmond in 1965 and relocated to Wimbledon in 1976, it is the only formal Buddhist temple, established according to Thai traditions, in the whole of Europe.

## 20–21. Camp Road & Camp View

Camp Road is one of the oldest streets in the Village area, and has played a significant part in its history. There has almost certainly been a hamlet located there, close to where the Fox and Grapes pub is today, since the medieval era. The street appears on the first detailed map of the Village, dated 1745, and since then it has been known by at least four different names.

The street is first named on a map in 1776, by which date it was known as Workhouse Lane. The Village's population had grown substantially in the first half of the 18th century, and as the population had grown so too had the challenges of homelessness and poverty. In 1752, the local Vestry, predecessor of today's local council, decided to build a workhouse to accommodate approximately 50 "impotent poor". They presumably picked Camp Road as the site for the workhouse to keep these impotent poor a respectable distance from the centre of the Village. The workhouse continued in operation until shortly after the Poor Law Amendment Act of 1834, after which time Wimbledon's poor were relocated to a larger workhouse in Kingston upon Thames.

In 1758, six years after the inception of the workhouse, a Free School was established on Workhouse Lane at the instigation of the vicar of St Mary's, John Cooksey, to provide a free education to local poor children, including those whose families were living in the nearby workhouse. This octagonal building survives today, and continues to be used as a school by The Study. In some records, the street was subsequently referred to as School Lane rather than Workhouse Lane.

In 1838, shortly after the workhouse had been decommissioned, a charity was created to build almshouses on the same site. The main instigator and benefactress of this charity was Charlotte Marryat, an American who lived in Wimbledon House on Parkside. Soon afterwards, Workhouse Lane (or School Lane) became known as Almshouse Lane, and the road retained this name until approximately 1900.

The first use of the name Camp Road appears in 1901. The name refers to Caesar's Camp on the Common. The origins of Caesar's Camp (which have nothing to do with Caesar) are described in the brief history at the start of this book. Sadly, Caesar's Camp was all but destroyed in 1875, but Camp Road played a big part in ensuring that the destruction of the Common was not a great deal worse. The landowner of the Old Park at that time was John Samuel Wanley Sawbridge-Erle-Drax, MP, ancestor of the Admiral Drax responsible for the subsequent development of the Old Park. Like his successor, John Sawbridge-Erle-Drax was keen to profit from his ownership of the Old Park, and had leased a sizeable chunk of his

*16. John Sawbridge-Erle-Drax, c1845. (Lithograph by an
unknown artist, from the collection of The Museum of
Wimbledon)*

land, including Caesar's Camp, to a builder called Mr Dixon, to develop houses. These plans met with significant local opposition, and happily these opponents succeeded in halting the development by persuading the courts to deny Drax's builder a right of access via Camp Road. Their victory came too late to save Caesar's Camp, which Drax and Dixon had by then razed to the ground in a spectacular act of archaeological vandalism.

Whereas Camp Road has a long history, Camp View was only developed in about 1884, shortly before the adjoining North View. Prior to that this area had been known as Croft's Fields. Henry Croft was a local resident who owned a timber yard on Camp Road.

## 22. Cannizaro Road

Cannizaro Road is named after Cannizaro House, and appears to have been created between 1745 (the date of the first detailed map of the Village, on which it does not appear) and 1776 (the date of a "Sketch of the Town of Wimbledon" made for the 1st Earl Spencer, on which it does appear). It originally ran from its current starting point off Parkside (by the site of the old animal pound) directly across the Common to the corner of Woodhayes Road. Its diversion via Cannizaro House originated in the mid-1850s.

Cannizaro House was originally known as Warren House. It was built in 1705, in conjunction with its neighbour Westside House, by William Browne, a London merchant. It was named Warren House because at that time the Old Park was known as The Warren, after Warren Farm, which was home to the warrener, who was the keeper of the rabbit warren on the Common, responsible for supplying the villagers with rabbit meat.

After William Browne's death the Old Park estate (including both Warren House and Westside House) had a succession of owners before passing via marriage to the Drax family in 1827. In 1817 Warren House had been leased by a Sicilian nobleman called Francis Platamone, Count St Antonio, and his Scottish wife Sophia Johnstone. Sophia was a great socialite, and passionately interested in music. She hosted frequent concerts in the house, attracting the great and the good of London society. The Count inherited the Dukedom of Cannizaro, a village in Sicily, in 1832. Shortly afterwards he abandoned Sophia to go and live in Italy. The Duchess of Cannizaro determinedly stayed put in the house until her sudden death in 1841. Her erstwhile husband died nine months later.

The name Cannizaro attached to Warren House, and then to Cannizaro Road, shortly after the Duchess's death, beginning with the census of 1841. The spelling of the name went through a variety of iterations (Cannazerro, Cennezero, Canazara) before Cannizaro was settled upon in 1874.

## 23. Carnegie Place

The late 1960s and early 1970s were low points in the naming of Wimbledon Village streets, both in terms of the selection of names and the public documentation of the reasons for these selections. This period gave the Village at least two streets (Alfreton Close and Welford Place), the names of which appear to have no connection with the history of Wimbledon. It also gave the Village Walham Rise, named after its developer, and Carnegie Place.

Carnegie Place was laid out in 1968. There are two possible Carnegies after whom it might have been named, but neither theory is entirely compelling. The first possibility is that it was named after the Honourable John Jarvis Carnegie, third son of the 7th Earl of Northesk. Carnegie's connection with Wimbledon was that, through his wife's inheritance, he owned the lease of Lauriston House on Southside. However, this theory is tenuous because Carnegie does not appear to have made any contribution to public life worthy of commemoration, and Carnegie Place is not close to Lauriston House.

The second Carnegie after whom Carnegie Place might have been named was Andrew Carnegie, the Scottish American industrialist who became one of the world's richest men and a leading philanthropist. Carnegie had no direct links with Wimbledon, but in 1928 the Carnegie UK Trust, which he had founded, was the largest donor to a fund created to lay out sports pitches on the Richardson Evans Memorial Playing Fields on the edge of the Common by Richmond Park. It is just possible that this act of philanthropy was recognised 40 years later in the naming of Carnegie Place, but again the rationale is not compelling.

## 24–25. Castle Close & Way

The Village has had a fort in Caesar's Camp, and practically had a palace in Cecil House, but it has never had a castle. Castle Close and Castle Way are both named after Castle Towers, which was a house that occupied 57 Parkside until it was demolished to make way for these two streets, which were laid out in 1959 and 1960.

In 1900 Castle Towers was for a while the temporary residence of Cecil Rhodes, the British imperialist and businessman after whom Rhodesia (now Zimbabwe) had been named five years earlier. Rhodes, who suffered from poor health for much of his life, had come from Africa to England to receive medical treatment. He may have chosen to stay in Wimbledon because Thomas Rudd, the brother of Rhodes' African business partner and chairman of the South African Goldfields Company, lived nearby in a house called The Keir on Westside.

For a large part of its life Castle Towers functioned as a hotel. Not much is known about its time as a hotel except that its most famous guest, in 1936, was Haile Selassie, Emperor of Ethiopia and messiah of the Rastafari movement. Haile Selassie had been forced to flee to the UK after the Italian invasion of his country, and he stayed in Castle Towers prior to moving as a guest into nearby Lincoln House (see entry for Lincoln Avenue).

Castle Towers thus had the distinction of having played host to both a leading proponent of European imperialism in Africa and one of its most steadfast opponents.

## 26. The Causeway

The road which we now know as The Causeway, running across the Common from the end of the High Street to Camp Road, first appears on a map of Wimbledon in 1776. By that date there was a well-established hamlet at Camp Road (or Workhouse Lane as it was then known) and The Causeway linked this hamlet to the Village.

The use of the name The Causeway for this road does not appear on maps until the middle of the 20th century.

A causeway is a raised track across boggy ground. We know that the Common used to be much boggier than is now the case. In 1864, when the 5th Earl Spencer announced a plan to enclose the Common, part of his proposition was that he would improve its quality by draining the boggier areas. Fortunately, his plans to deprive Wimbledon residents of open access to the Common were thwarted (see the entry for Peek Crescent).

The word causeway derives from a Middle English word 'causey' (an archaic form of causeway) which came from the French word 'causee', which was itself derived from the Latin word for limestone, 'calx'. Limestone was a material commonly used by the Romans to pave tracks.

# 27. Cedar Court

Cedar Court is one of four streets in the Village to be named after cedar trees (the others being Cedarland Terrace, Cedar Park Gardens and High Cedar Drive). Cedars are the trees most frequently referred to in the street names of the Village. There are also two streets named after oak trees, and one each for sycamore, beech and walnut trees. The prevalence of cedar trees in the Village, and hence in the Village's street names, reflects the popularity that these trees enjoyed amongst the designers of fine gardens in the 18th and 19th centuries.

Cedars are not native to the UK. The first cedar tree recorded in England was planted in Oxfordshire by the Reverend Edward Pocock in 1642. The first tree to yield seeds was planted in the Chelsea Physic Garden in 1732. The popularity of planting cedars in the grounds of large houses started at about the same time, and was sustained throughout the rest of the 18th century by garden designers such as William Kent, Humphrey Repton and Capability Brown. The Cedar of Lebanon was the cedar of choice until the mid-19th century when two further varieties, the Atlas and the Deodar, were introduced to England. The popularity of planting cedars began to wane after the 1840s, partly due to the introduction of the giant evergreens of North America such as redwoods and sequoias. There remains one large cedar tree in Cedar Court, best seen from Burghley Road.

Cedar Court was developed in 1968, and was named after a house on the site of the same name. This house had, for many years, been used as a residential English language school by an international Catholic lay organisation called the Teresian Association. This organisation (named after St Teresa of Avila) was founded in 1911 by St Pedro Poveda, a Spanish priest subsequently martyred in the Spanish Civil War, and has as its objective "the human promotion of individuals and the transformation of unjust structures by means of an education and culture imparted from the platform of Christianity". In 1962 the Teresian Association relocated to new premises in Kingston upon Thames.

## 28. Cedarland Terrace

Cedarland Terrace was laid out off Copse Hill in 1986. Like nearby High Cedar Drive, Cedarland Terrace benefits from the presence of several cedar trees which survive in what were the grounds of the larger houses that used to grace Copse Hill, in particular Prospect Place (see entry for Prospect Place).

## 29. Cedar Park Gardens

Cedar Park Gardens has the distinction of being one of only three Village streets to have been laid out in the 21st century (the others being Atkinson Close and Rydon Mews). It was developed in 2005 in the grounds of the house that had occupied 35 Camp Road. This house, originally known as The Rounds, had been renamed By Caesar's Camp in 1906 by Sir George Stegman Gibb, managing director of what is now the London Underground. Sir George and his family lived in By Caesar's Camp until 1919. The house had several further owners prior to its demolition in 1959 to make way for offices, which were in turn demolished to make way for the houses of Cedar Park Gardens.

On acquiring By Caesar's Camp, Sir George had commissioned one of England's best-known landscape gardeners to re-design its surrounds. Gertrude Jekyll was a very eminent Victorian. Born in 1843, she trained as an artist, exhibited at the Royal Academy, and mastered a wide range of other artistic accomplishments before settling upon garden design as her preferred creative outlet. Over a period of 35 years Jekyll designed some 400 gardens, including many in collaboration with architect Sir Edwin Lutyens. In her twilight years

Jekyll's portrait was painted by the celebrated artist William Nicholson. He made a separate painting of her gardening boots, which were reputed to be some 40 years old. Jekyll wrote of these boots "no house painter likes a new brush . . . I suppose no horse likes a new collar . . . I am quite sure I do not like new boots". On her death at the age of 89 Lutyens designed her tombstone with the inscription 'Gertrude Jekyll – artist, gardener, craftswoman'.

Sadly, most of Gertrude Jekyll's garden at 35 Camp Road has long since been built upon, but at least a couple of her cedar trees do survive, justifying the naming of Cedar Park Gardens.

## 30. Chester Road

Chester Road was laid out in 1956, and is named after nearby Chester House, which was built in 1680 and is the fourth oldest house in the Village (after the Old Rectory, Eagle House and Claremont House). The original ownership of Chester House is uncertain. There is a legend that it was built by James, Duke of York (subsequently King James II) for one of his mistresses. The evidence for this theory is thin, and rests on the presence in St Mary's churchyard of the grave of their alleged offspring, one John Fitzjames. It is also speculated that the first occupant was Benjamin Lordell, a wealthy London merchant whose trade was conducted in Oporto, Portugal. Again, there appears to be little evidence for this claim, and it is known that Lordell lived for a while in another house on Southside called Oakholm. The origin of the name Chester House is also uncertain. One theory is that it may have been named in the 18th century by Thomas Grosvenor, who in 1769 inherited the Old Park estate on which Chester House was located, and who was MP for the city of Chester.

What is known for certain is that Chester House's most famous resident was another MP, John Horne Tooke, who lived there from 1782 to 1812. Horne Tooke was a radical politician who devoted his political career to agitating for parliamentary reform and who, like his acolyte Sir Francis Burdett who lived in nearby Wimbledon Villa, was twice imprisoned for his efforts. He was first incarcerated in 1777 for supporting the Americans during the American War of Independence. In 1794

*17. John Horne Tooke, 1791. (Line engraving by Anker Smith, after Thomas Hardy, © National Portrait Gallery, London)*

he was sent to the Tower of London (a feat that Sir Francis Burdett was subsequently to emulate) on suspicion of treason in connection with his support of the French Revolution. Happily he was acquitted at trial, and was able to live out his days at Chester House. Some years before his death in 1812 he arranged for a vault to be excavated in the garden of Chester House for his own burial. At the time of his death the vault was flooded, and so he had to be buried elsewhere.

## 31–32. Church Hill & Road

These two streets are both named after St Mary's Church which, sitting as it does at the apex of Church Road, has its fortnight of glory every summer when no BBC broadcast of the tennis is complete without at least one shot of the spire of St Mary's on the horizon. A brief history of St Mary's Church is given under St Mary's Road.

Church Hill was laid out in the last quarter of the 19th century. Church Road is considerably older. It was certainly laid out by 1720, and probably much earlier. In an 'Exact Survey' of 1720, which may have been commissioned by Sarah Churchill, Duchess of Marlborough before she built Wimbledon's third manor house, Church Road is described as Wimbledon Lane. By the middle of the 19th century, Church Road as we know it today was regarded as three separate roads; Park Road (at the Southfields end), Church Road (leading up to the church) and Church Street (from the church to the High Street). First Church Street in 1879 and then Park Road in 1921 were merged into Church Road, and in that latter year an adjunct of Church Road was renamed St Mary's Road.

Since 1922 Church Road has been home to the All England Lawn Tennis & Croquet Club, the venue of the Wimbledon Tennis Championship for which Wimbledon is known throughout the world. The club was originally founded as a croquet club in 1868 by John Walsh, editor of The Field maga-

73

zine, and was based in a field off Worple Road, just outside the Village. In 1875, with the craze for croquet waning, the club's committee took the foresighted decision to make over one croquet lawn to the new game of lawn tennis which had been codified by Major Walter Clopton Wingfield only the previous year. The game instantly took off, and in 1877 the club held the first open championship, instructing that "players must provide their own rackets and must wear shoes without heels". This inaugural tournament was won by local boy Spencer Gore, whose family was related to Earl Spencer, and who had been born and brought up in Westside House on Westside. The championship rapidly grew in popularity, and by 1922 the Worple Road premises had become too small, prompting the club to move to its current grounds in Church Road.

## 33. Clement Road

Clement Road was laid out in 1905 as part of the development of the Belvedere estate. It was named after Clement Peache (1747–1815), who was the great-grandfather of the James Courthope Peache who sold the Belvedere estate for development, and the father of the James Courthope Peache who had originally acquired and named Belvedere House.

Like his son, Clement was a shipwright in Lambeth. He married Elizabeth Courthope in 1776. It seems likely that he founded the family business that enabled his son to prosper and purchase Belvedere House. Clement is buried in the graveyard of St John's Church in Waterloo, along with Elizabeth and eight other family members, in a large tomb erected by his son.

## 34. Clifton Road

Clifton Road is one of the five interconnecting roads between the Ridgway and Southside that were all laid out in a 50-year period ending with the development of Murray Road in 1907.

Clifton Road was laid out at the beginning of the 1880s, and Clifton House at the Southside end of the road was built at the same time.

The development of both Clifton House and Clifton Road was the responsibility of the Oliver family. The Olivers, who were already a wealthy family, owning several properties in Wimbledon including Oliver's House at the Southside end of what was to become Clifton Road, became an extremely wealthy family when they inherited the estate of an aunt, Margaret Whately, who died in 1872. Margaret Whately, who lived in the affluent Bristol suburb of Clifton Down, left the Oliver family an estate of some 50 freehold properties in nearby Clifton Park. It was this bequest which led to the naming of Clifton House and Road.

Margaret Whately's nephew and beneficiary, William Elliott Oliver, died shortly after his aunt in 1877. It was William's widow, Elizabeth Oliver, who was responsible for the development of Clifton Road and the building of Clifton House. Elizabeth entered into an agreement in 1878 with her Southside neighbour, Edward Mansel, under which she took responsibility for laying out Clifton Road. The road was completed in 1880, and between 1880 and 1885 Elizabeth sold off plots of land to the east side of Clifton Road for residential development. Clifton House was completed at the same time, and in 1883 Elizabeth entered into an agreement to lease the house to a local builder, Tom Plumtree. Elizabeth died seven years later in 1890.

Clifton House was badly damaged by a bomb on 19th February 1944. It was substantially rebuilt and converted into four flats in 1956.

## 35. Clockhouse Close

Clockhouse Close was named after Clock House which, slightly confusingly, was a house on the adjacent Windmill

Road. The original Clock House was built in approximately 1800 by one Arthur Tyton, who had obtained permission from Earl Spencer to build on the edge of the Common. Arthur Tyton was a lawyer by profession who served for 55 years as a solicitor to His Majesty's Customs. He is remembered not for his professional career but for his hobby. In the words of his obituary he was a "venerable and well-known collector of the topography and antiquities of the county of Surrey", who by his death in 1832 had amassed an unrivalled collection of prints and drawings. His hobby may have had an influence on his character, or vice versa, for his obituary also describes him as "singular and somewhat blunt in his manners".

Arthur Tyton's house was demolished and a second house of the same name constructed in 1888. This second house was badly damaged by a bomb in 1944, but was subsequently repaired and in 1956 it became the Vietnamese Embassy. The house was eventually demolished in approximately 1990, and replaced with a block of flats which is also called Clockhouse.

To add to the slight confusion over names, Windmill Road was originally known as Clockhouse Road, and was not renamed Windmill Road until early in the 20th century. The current Clockhouse Close was laid out in 1983 in the grounds of what had been Clock House.

## 36. Coach House Lane

Coach House Lane was developed in 1967 on the site of what had been the coach house of Atherton Grange. Atherton Grange had been built somewhere between 1850 and 1869 on land sold off by John Augustus Beaumont. Some of Atherton Grange's more characterful residents are described under the entry for Atherton Drive.

## 37. Copse Hill

Copse Hill is one of the oldest roads in Wimbledon. As a continuation of the Ridgway, in the medieval era it was the main route to Wimbledon's nearest market town, Kingston upon Thames. For many centuries Copse Hill was an uninhabited lane leading through woods. The colonisation of Copse Hill began in about 1757 when Peter Taylor, a London goldsmith, built a large house called Prospect Place close to the site of what became Atkinson Morley's Hospital. Prospect Place (see the entry for the Prospect Place), became one of the five large estates (in conjunction with Wimbledon Park, Wimbledon House, Belvedere and Old Park) the break-up and development of which subsequently shaped the modern Village. Copse Hill is referred to by name in rate books of 1838, in the census of 1865 and on the Ordnance Survey map of 1876.

Copse Hill is named for the woods through which it used to run. Prior to their development, the woods to the north of Copse Hill were part of the Old Park, the estate owned after 1827 by the Drax family. To the south of Copse Hill, the woods were known as 'the Wild Land' because they had not been under cultivation since the Middle Ages.

Copse is a shortening of the word coppice, which refers to an area of woodland where the trees are periodically cut back to ground level to provide timber for firewood, fencing and building. The word coppice comes from the French word couper, to cut.

Copse Hill remained largely undeveloped until the beginning of the 20th century. Local resident Mrs Hester Thackery Fuller recalled that in 1900 it was "a lonely lane winding its way down through the hazel woods to Coombe". The widening of Copse Hill took place in 1925 to facilitate the development by the Drax family of the Old Park estate.

*18. Copse Hill, c1905. (Postcard published by The Collectors'*
*Publishing Company, London, from the author's collection)*

## 38–40. Cottenham Drive, Park Road & Place

The development of that part of the Village which lies to the south of Copse Hill, including the three Cottenham roads, took place primarily on the Prospect Place estate (see the entry for Prospect Place).

In 1831 Prospect Place was purchased by Charles Pepys, a Whig politician and indirect descendant of the famous diarist. Contemporary accounts indicate that Pepys was an unremarkable lawyer and a charmless individual. In 1836, however, the Prime Minister, Lord Melbourne, made him Lord Chancellor and elevated him to the peerage with the title Baron Cottenham, later Earl of Cottenham, in the county of Cambridge. The diarist Charles Greville described the promotion of this "plain, undistinguished man" as "one of the most curious instances of elevation that ever occurred". Another contemporary, Lord Kingsdown, wrote that "Melbourne must have felt very much like a man who had parted with a brilliant capricious mistress [the previous Lord Chancellor] and married his housekeeper".

Cottenham is a village in Cambridgeshire close to the Fens, and was the ancestral home of the Pepys family. It is otherwise best known for the Great Fire of Cottenham, which occurred in 1850, a year before Pepys' death, and which destroyed much of the village.

Pepys died in 1851 and his family subsequently sold off much of the Prospect Place estate to developers, who named two principal roads across the estate in his honour (Cottenham Park Road, which is within the Village, and Pepys Road which lies just outside the Village boundary.) The residential development of these roads and the rest of the Prospect Place estate gained real momentum after the opening of Raynes Park station in 1871.

Cottenham Drive and Cottenham Place were developed much more recently in 1960.

*19. Cottenham Park Road, c1911. (Postcard published by The Collectors' Publishing Company, London, from the author's collection)*

# 41. Courthope Road

Courthope Road was part of the Belvedere estate which had been purchased by James Courthope Peache in 1834. It is named after his mother whose maiden name was Elizabeth Courthope. Elizabeth was born in 1750, married James's father Clement Peache in 1776, and bore three surviving children. She died in 1830 at the age of 80, and is buried alongside Clement and eight other members of her family in the graveyard of St John's Church in Waterloo.

Courthope Road was developed in approximately 1874 when the Belvedere estate was jointly owned by James Courthope Peache's two surviving children, Alfred and Kezia Peache. Alfred had joined the clergy and had moved away from Wimbledon leaving Kezia, who never married, in sole possession of Belvedere House. Kezia lived in Wimbledon until her death in 1899 and made a great contribution to

Wimbledon life. She was organist at St Mary's Church, taught in the Sunday school, and was a benefactress of many charitable activities in the Village. In particular, Kezia was a generous donor to the Cottage Improvement Society, founded in 1859 to provide "good, suitable dwellings for the working classes at a moderate rent". In total, she was responsible for the building of nearly 50 workers' cottages in Wimbledon, including both Courthope Villas and Bertram Cottages in the town centre.

## 42. Cranford Close

Cranford Close was laid out in 1961, shortly after nearby Cottenham Drive and Cottenham Place, on the site of a Victorian house named Cranford.

The house is thought to have been named Cranford after the highly popular novel of the same name, written by Elizabeth Gaskell in 1851. Set in Knutsford, Cheshire, 'Cranford' is a gentle satire on the efforts of a fading, genteel society to resist the changes being forced upon it by the industrial revolution.

There are two links between 'Cranford' and Wimbledon. The first is that Elizabeth Gaskell's daughter, Marianne, became a Wimbledon resident having married Edward Thurstan Holland (her second cousin), founder of Wimbledon Hospital (see the entry for Thurstan Road). The second link relates to the illustrations that populated the best-known edition of 'Cranford'. These were the work of an Irish-born illustrator called Hugh Thomson. His depictions in the book of Cheshire scenery were much praised, "which amused me very much, for as a matter of fact I had never seen it, having really done my country sketches from studies I had made on Wimbledon Common".

Cranford Close is one of two streets in the Village to be named after a popular novel, the other one being Windy Ridge Close.

## 43. Crooked Billet

Crooked Billet is named after the pub of the same name. There is a legend, for which there is no evidence, that this pub was once owned by William Cromwell, father of Henry VIII's chief minister, Thomas Cromwell.

The first houses at the Crooked Billet were probably built in the late 17th century at about the same time as nearby Chester House. The first named reference to the Crooked Billet alehouse was in 1745. A crooked billet was a staff used by shepherds to tend their flocks. The name therefore harks back to a time when the Common was used to graze sheep. Today the Crooked Billet and its near neighbour the Hand in Hand are both Youngs pubs, but the Crooked Billet's best-known resident was the founding father of the rival brewery, Watneys.

*20. Crooked Billet, 1913. (Photograph by Cicely Cardew, from the collection of The Museum of Wimbledon)*

Daniel Watney was born in 1705, and legend has it that he was abandoned by Gypsies on Wimbledon Common and was taken in by local farmer Joseph Acres, whose daughter Mary he subsequently married. Daniel went on to become a successful farmer, and he used the profits of his labour to buy up many of the cottages on and around the Crooked Billet. He and Mary had four surviving children, all of whom prospered; two sons also became farmers (one taking on Warren Farm on the Common), a third son established a brewery west of the Crooked Billet and their daughter, Mary, married Samuel Mason, landlord of the Rose & Crown pub on the other side of the Common. It was Daniel's great-grandson, James Watney, who was responsible for investing in 1837 in the business that was to become Watneys.

## 44. Currie Hill Close

Currie Hill Close was developed in 1956 on the site of Currie Hill House, after which the street was named. Currie Hill House had been built in the 1880s by John Carr on land purchased in 1875 from John Augustus Beaumont for the sum of £4,100. It is not known why John Carr chose the name Currie Hill for his house. There is a Curriehill House in Currie on the outskirts of Edinburgh, built in 1856 by Lord Curriehill, a Scottish Law Lord. It is possible that John Carr, who had lived for much of his life in Carlisle, had some connection or affinity with Curriehill.

John Carr may have left no clues to the name of his house, but he did leave at least one substantial gift to posterity, for he was the inventor of the Garibaldi biscuit. John Carr was a biscuit maker, who had learnt his trade working in his elder brother's business, Carr's of Carlisle, makers of the celebrated water biscuit. John Carr worked in Carlisle for 20 years, but eventually grew frustrated at his brother's failure to share responsibility for the running of the business, and left with a generous pay-off of £7,000 for his share of the business. Soon afterwards, Carr was approached by James Peek, a wealthy tea importer who had decided to diversify into biscuit making in partnership with his niece's husband, George Frean. Peek Frean was established in 1857, John Carr came down to London to join the business, and shortly afterwards in 1861 he invented the Garibaldi biscuit (named after the Italian general who had made a popular visit to Britain in 1854). John Carr was the first biscuit maker to succeed in making mass-market biscuits that were not rock hard, and his innovations were responsible for the great success of the Peek Frean business.

In addition to Currie Hill Close, John Carr's creative biscuit-making skills were to lead to the naming of at least two further Wimbledon streets. John's son, Arthur Carr, who followed in his father's footsteps and ultimately became chairman of Peek Frean, was to commission another house in the Village which was subsequently named Windyridge, ultimately spawning the street Windy Ridge Close. Meanwhile, James Peek's son was Sir Henry Peek, MP, who was to sell off the Wimbledon House estate for development, spawning several new roads, including Peek Crescent.

## 45. Dairy Walk

Today Dairy Walk is an overgrown and overlooked footpath that runs off Church Road between Burghley Road and Somerset Road, emerging opposite Atherton Drive. It is included in this survey of Village streets because it has been a public right of way for many centuries. It was named Dairy Walk because it used to link St Mary's Church and the Old Rectory with Dairy Farm which was located on the edge of the Wimbledon Park estate. In 1883 John Augustus Beaumont, who had purchased the Wimbledon Park estate in 1846, sold the Dairy Farm to Sir Henry Peek, owner of the adjacent Wimbledon House estate. Some of Dairy Farm's fields subsequently made up part of the land purchased in 1922 by the All England Lawn Tennis & Croquet Club.

## 46. Deepdale

Deepdale was developed in 1957 in conjunction with two adjacent roads, Margin Drive and Windy Ridge Close. The three roads were laid out and eponymously named in the grounds of three houses called Deepdale, Margin House and Windyridge. The name Deepdale reflects the local geography because the house was indeed located at the bottom of a relatively deep dale.

Deepdale had been a large house set in six acres. Along with Margin House and Windyridge it was requisitioned for the war effort in 1939. The three houses were not released back to their owners until the early 1950s, by which time they were in such a state of disrepair that the owners decided to sell out to a local builder who, after overcoming the objections of 87 other property owners on the Wimbledon House estate, consolidated the three houses and their grounds into a 16-acre site for residential development.

## 47. Drax Avenue

Drax Avenue sits on the Old Park estate, first mentioned under Almer Road, which was owned by the Drax family. It was developed in 1926 by the then head of the family, Admiral the Honourable Sir Reginald Aylmer Ranfurly Plunkett-Ernle-Erle-Drax.

The Admiral's impressive quadruple-barrelled surname had evolved over several centuries reflecting a tendency amongst his ancestors to produce only female heirs. Four barrels should be enough for any surname, but the Drax family might have had a fifth, for the first family in the Admiral's ancestry to spawn a female heir was the Wykes family. The Wykes family were the owners of Charborough House in Dorset (close to the village of Almer) when, in 1549, the heiress Mary Wykes married Walter Erle. The Wykes surname did not survive the marriage, and hence it was Erle that became the first barrel of the surviving surname.

The best-known Erle was Walter's grandson, also Walter, who was a soldier in early life and an active parliamentarian in later life, and who combined both interests by leading the Parliamentary forces that besieged Corfe Castle in the Civil War.

The Drax surname entered the fray in 1720 when Henry Drax of Ellerton Abbey in Yorkshire (see the entry for Ellerton Road) married the second Walter's great-granddaughter and heiress, Elizabeth. Henry appears to have retained his own surname, but their children were given the surname Erle-Drax.

The Drax family, originally from Normandy, had come to England with King Henry II in 1154. By the time that Henry married Elizabeth the wealth of the Drax family was more than a match for the landed estates of the Erle family. The Drax's family fortune had been created in the 17th century by Henry's great-grandfather, James Drax, who had emigrated to Barbados in 1629 and accumulated huge wealth by pioneering the development of sugar plantations and investing the proceeds in the emerging slave trade. James Drax had returned to England in the 1650s to receive a knighthood from Oliver Cromwell for his part in rescuing Barbados from the royalists, and to invest his extensive fortune in acquiring a series of estates throughout the country.

The Drax family still live at Charborough House in Dorset, and continue to own Drax Hall in Barbados, which is reputed to be the oldest Jacobean mansion in the New World. The current head of the family, Richard Drax, is at least the seventh member of his family to have become an MP. The origins of the remaining two barrels of the Drax family's extended sur-

*21. Admiral the Honourable Sir Reginald Aylmer Ranfurly Plunkett-Ernle-Erle-Drax, 1918. (Vintage print by George Charles Beresford, © National Portrait Gallery, London)*

name, Plunkett and Ernle, are described under the entries for Dunstall Road and Ernle Road respectively.

## 48. Draxmont

Draxmont was a large house on Wimbledon Hill Road (hence the 'mont') owned by the Drax family. It was built in the second half of the 19th century. It was converted into a hotel in 1932, and remained in operation for nearly 40 years. In 1971 the hotel was closed and in the following year it was sold for £205,000 to a developer who demolished it to build a block of flats. The small road leading to Draxmont was originally named Draxmont Approach. It became Draxmont in 1953 when the Council allocated street numbers to the road, designating the hotel Number 1 Draxmont.

The last occupants of Draxmont prior to its conversion to a hotel had been Sir Henry and Lady Annie Holloway. Sir Henry had been chairman of the eponymous building company Holloway Brothers (ultimately acquired by John Laing & Son in 1964) and had been knighted in 1917 for the part that he had played in solving the urgent need to create housing for the workers in Britain's wartime factories.

## 49. Dunstall Road

Dunstall Road is another product of the Drax family's development of the Old Park estate, and was laid out, in conjunction with McKay Road and Wool Road, in 1928–29. The builder was AJ Styles of Ernle Road, and the initial cost was £1,675 for a four-bedroom house and £2,400 for a five-bedder.

Dunstall Road was named after Dunstall Priory, a family home in Shoreham, Kent, belonging to the Plunkett family. Plunkett was the final barrel to be bolted onto the Drax family's quadruple-barrelled surname, and was Admiral Drax's own family name. The Admiral was the younger son of John Plunkett, 17th Baron of Dunsany in Ireland, who had married his second cousin Ernle Elizabeth Louisa Mary Grosvenor Burton (later Ernle-Erle-Drax). Ernle (whose unusual first name was taken from her ancestress, Elizabeth Ernle) was herself the daughter of another Plunkett, Colonel Francis Augustus Plunkett Burton, who had married Sarah Frances Elizabeth Ernle-Erle-Drax, another Drax family heiress (daughter to John Samuel Wanley Sawbridge-Erle-Drax). The level of complexity inherent in the Drax family tree due to the preponderance of female heirs has been compounded over the centuries by the tendency of family members to marry their cousins. The Admiral could have simplified matters by sticking to his father's one-barrelled surname (Plunkett), but in 1916 he elected to change his surname by Royal Licence to Plunkett-Ernle-Erle-Drax.

Dunstall Priory was built as a private house in 1810, and was the Dunsany's family home in England. After the death of Admiral Drax's mother in 1916, it was occupied by his elder brother, Edward Plunkett, 18th Baron of Dunsany, who was a well-known writer, publishing over 80 books, many of them fantasy stories. Edward might have been Dunstall Priory's most prolific author, but he was not the most prestigious, for during the Second World War the house was home to Anthony Powell, author of the celebrated 12 volume cycle of novels 'A Dance to the Music of Time'.

## 50. Ellerton Road

Laid out in 1926, Ellerton Road was also developed by the Drax family on the Old Park estate. The name refers to Ellerton Abbey, a regency villa built by the Drax family in about 1830 as a shooting lodge close to the River Swale in North Yorkshire.

The Ellerton estate has a lengthy history, and was listed in the Domesday Book, when its taxable value was deemed to be two geld units. Ellerton was recorded as having belonged to Gamal, son of Karli, in 1066. By 1086 when the Domesday Book was compiled, following the Norman invasion, the owner was Count Alan of Brittany.

In the late 12th century a priory of Cistercian nuns was established at Ellerton. The priory was badly damaged by marauding Scots in 1342, and its dissolution was completed by Henry VIII in 1535. The Ellerton estate passed into the owner-ship of the Drax family some years later in 1581 when Gabriel Drax purchased Ellerton Abbey, which is now a ruin in the grounds of the Ellerton Abbey house.

## 51. Ernle Road

Yet another road on the Drax family's empire, Ernle Road was developed in 1926, although maps show a path running along the route of Ernle Road at least as early as 1850.

Ernle Road commemorates another branch of the Drax family tree, and enables us to complete the saga of Admiral the Honourable Sir Reginald Aylmer Ranfurly Plunkett-Ernle-Erle-Drax's quadruple-barrelled surname.

The first known member of the Ernle family, at the end of the 12th century, was Luke de Ernle of the Sussex parish of Earnley (which is how the surname should be pronounced). An Ernle baronetcy (which subsequently lapsed) was created in 1661 for Walter Ernle, later MP for Devizes.

The Ernle surname first crossed paths with the Erle family (which constituted the original barrel of the quadruple-barrelled surname) at the end of the 17th century when Frances Erle of Charborough (heiress to General Thomas Erle) married Sir Edward Ernle (the 3rd baronet). It was their daughter and heiress, Elizabeth Ernle, who introduced the Drax barrel to the surname by marrying Henry Drax in 1720. Elizabeth and Henry's children took the surname Erle-Drax, and hence the Ernle barrel fell away for the next few generations.

For reasons which are not entirely clear, the Ernle surname was reinstated in the extended family name by the Admiral's grandmother. She took a belt and braces approach when naming her daughter by giving her Ernle as a first name as well as a surname. Hence, Admiral Drax's mother rejoiced (or possibly not) in the name Ernle Elizabeth Louisa Mary Grosvenor Ernle-Erle-Drax. Compared to his mother's name, the Admiral's moniker seems positively modest.

## 52. Eversley Park

Eversley Park is a modern development, laid out off Camp Road in 1982. It is named after George John Shaw-Lefevre, 1st Baron Eversley, who for a time lived nearby in Westside House.

Eversley was a Liberal politician who served in the governments of two Prime Ministers, Lord Russell and William Gladstone. He is aptly commemorated in Wimbledon because of the role that he played in helping to conserve Wimbledon Common in the 1860s, and in promoting the conservation of green spaces more generally.

The story of how Wimbledon Common came under threat in the 1860s, when the 5th Earl Spencer hatched a plan to enclose it, is described more fully under the entry for Peek Crescent because of the prominent role that Sir Henry Peek, MP, played in leading the opposition to the lord of the manor's unpalatable plan. Lord Eversley sat on the Commons Select Committee which investigated the proposal and ultimately found against Earl Spencer.

Lord Eversley was inspired by the case of Wimbledon Common to help found in 1865 the Commons Preservation Society, which can justly claim to be the UK's oldest conservation charity. Now known as the Open Spaces Society, in 2015 it celebrated 150 years of campaigning for Britain's commons, greens and public footpaths. Lord Eversley was

91

*22. John Poyntz Spencer, 5th Earl Spencer, 1903. (Sepia-toned platinotype print by George Charles Beresford, © National Portrait Gallery, London)*

chairman of the Society, a position that he held almost continuously until his death in 1928 at the age of 96.

There was an irony in the role that Lord Eversley played in thwarting Earl Spencer's plans to develop Wimbledon Common, for as an aspiring young lawyer Eversley's father, John Shaw-Lefevre, had built a successful law practice primarily by acting as property conveyancer for Earl Spencer.

## 53. Gibbard Mews

Gibbard Mews was created at 37 High Street in 1976 at the time of the development of Woodcock House, the main building in the Mews.

Gibbard Mews is named after the Gibbard family that had lived at 37 High Street for many years. The Gibbards were builders and property developers, trading under the name of Gibbard & Son. The family business had been founded in the late 19th century by Thomas Gibbard. The business passed through two further generations of the Gibbard family before being wound up in 1970.

The development of Woodcock House and Gibbard Mews was completed later in the 1970s by another family business of builders and property developers, Woodcock Brothers. The founding father of the Woodcock dynasty was Wally Woodcock, who had started in the building trade shortly before the Second World War. Like the Gibbard business before it, the Woodcock business is now in the hands of a third generation, and it continues to operate from Woodcock House in Gibbard Mews.

## 54. Glencairn Road

Glencairn Road, which leads off the Ridgway into King's College School, is named after Glencairn House which is located just before the entrance to the school. This house, which was designed by Robert Roumieu, a well-known architect of Huguenot descent, and built in 1866, was originally known as Ridgway Paddocks.

The house was renamed Glencairn House by a later occupant, Charles Shipley Gordon, who moved into the house in approximately 1890. Gordon, who was a wine merchant, named the house after the Earls of Glencairn, to whom his mother was related. The parish of Glencairn is situated in Dumfries and Galloway in Scotland. It takes its name from Cairn Water, a small river that runs through the parish. Glencairn Castle dates back to 1370. There had been Earls of Glencairn from 1488 until 1796, when the title had become dormant on the death of the 15th Earl.

By 1913 Glencairn House was owned by Fred Carrodus, a science teacher at KCS. In that year, he let the house to the school, and for the next 35 years it functioned as the school's boarding house. When the lease expired in 1948, the school decided not to pay the purchase price asked for the house, and so it reverted to the Carrodus family.

In the Second World War, Glencairn House was bombed on 18th February 1944. The KCS housemaster at the time, CH Dann, wrote that "at the moment of impact every boy was at his bedside, that is within three feet of the walls, and not a boy was hurt as much as a scratch, though the roof fell in. I have always believed in miracles!"

## 55. The Grange

The Grange is one of the five interconnecting roads between the Ridgway and Southside that were all laid out in a 50 year period ending with the development of Murray Road in 1907. The Grange was laid out in the 1880s, and was named after a new house of the same name which fronted onto Southside.

The first house to be built on this site was completed in 1747, and was known as Wimbledon Villa. This house was one of a number of grand houses to be built on Southside in the first half of the 18th century. Others included Lingfield House (1715), Laurel House (1724, subsequently Lauriston House) and Southside House (1751).

The first occupant of Wimbledon Villa was one Thomas Lewis, of whom little is known. Subsequent notable occupants included the Duke of Newcastle, the Countess of Bristol, Sir Francis Burdett, MP (see entry for Burdett Avenue), and Sir Richard Garth, MP. The last of these, Sir Richard, was by inheritance the Lord of the Manor of Morden. Sir Richard captained Oxford University at cricket, trained as a barrister, became Chief Justice of Bengal and MP for Guildford. For all of this his name is commemorated by Garth Road in Morden, host to both a cemetery and a recycling centre.

Throughout this time the freehold of Wimbledon Villa was owned by the descendants of John 'Vulture' Hopkins. Hopkins was a banker who had purchased Wimbledon House on Parkside in the early 1720s and subsequently acquired and developed large chunks of land along Southside, Ridgway and Worple Road. Hopkins's nickname and reputation confirms that the current disdain for bankers is not a new phenomenon. The contemporary poet John Gay wrote of him that he'd "ruin thousands for a single groat", and fellow satirist Alexander Pope opined that he "lived worthless, but died worth £300,000".

On John Hopkins's death in 1732, without immediate heirs, his estate ultimately passed to a distant cousin, Benjamin Bond, who changed his surname to Bond-Hopkins in honour of his wealthy benefactor. On Benjamin's death in 1794 the estate passed to his daughter, Caroline Hopkins, and when Caroline married Sir Richard Mansel Phillips, MP, in 1797 the estate passed into the hands of the Mansel Phillips family.

The estate was still in the hands of this family almost a century later when, in 1887, financial difficulties forced descendant Sir Richard Mansel to put the house and its grounds up for sale. Sir Richard initially tried to sell the entire estate in one go, but he was unable to find a buyer and so the street was laid out and the estate sold off in lots at auction. The majority of the lots were bought by Sir Henry Peek (see entry for Peek Crescent) and two builders. Between them they subsequently developed 23 houses on the 48 lots.

Wimbledon Villa itself was demolished shortly afterwards in 1887, and a new house, The Grange, was built in its place. The street was known as Grange Road on a map of 1890, but as The Grange on a map of 1894 and on subsequent maps.

## 56. Grange Park Place

Grange Park Place was developed in 1985 on the site of the former Wimbledon Hospital at the end of Thurstan Road. A brief history of the hospital is given under the entry for Thurstan Road. The hospital was closed down in 1983, and in the following year the NHS sold the site for residential development to builders McAlpine Homes for £1.8 million.

Before the building of the hospital in 1870 the land now occupied by Grange Park Place had been woodland. In the 17th century it was known as Brooms Down Wood, and in the 18th century both as Heavon's Wood and Broomfield Wood. By the 19th century it was simply known as Wimbledon Wood.

There is no historical record of this site ever having been known as Grange Park. However, in medieval records Wimbledon as a whole was described as a grange within the manor of Mortlake. A grange was an outlying farm, typically belonging to a monastery or feudal lord. It was because of Wimbledon's status as an adjunct to the manor of Mortlake that it did not merit a separate entry in the Domesday Book compiled in 1086. Hence, whilst it may not have been deliberate on the part of the developers, the name Grange Park Place can be said to hark back to Wimbledon's earliest documented history.

## 57. The Green

The description of a patch of grassy land close to a village as a green first appears in the English language in 1477. The use of this term for the road in Wimbledon that we now know as The Green was not adopted until much later.

This corner of the Common appears to have been first occupied in the mid-17th century. At that time The Green was known as "The Little Common Garden". This patch of land, including one cottage, was purchased in 1676 by Edward West, a local farmer, for £84.

Over a century later, in 1782, The Green, which by this time held two substantial houses, was acquired and further developed by Samuel Mason, landlord of The Rose & Crown. This transaction is described in more detail in the entry for nearby Mason's Yard.

In 1902 The Green (which at that time was still known by many locals as the "Old Pound Patch" because it had previously been the site of the village pound where stray animals were contained) was the subject of further proposed residential development, prompting substantial local opposition. The Wimbledon House Estate Company, which had recently purchased Wimbledon House and its estate on the death of Sir Henry Peek, announced its intention to build a block of flats on The Green. Opposition to this proposal led local worthies to found, in 1903, the John Evelyn Club (now the Wimbledon Society) "to safeguard the amenities of the district, to promote an interest in local history and wildlife, and to preserve objects of historical and natural interest". The lobbying of these individuals was partially successful, resulting in the proposed development being stepped down from a block of flats to three houses.

The Green's most famous resident was perhaps Sir William Congreve (1772–1828) who lived at 1 The Green. Sir William, who was the son of the Comptroller of the Royal Laboratories

***23. Sir William Congreve, c1812. (Oil on canvas by James
Lonsdale, © National Portrait Gallery, London)***

at Woolwich Arsenal (a position which he too would ultimately
hold) was an inveterate inventor who developed a rocket for
military use, which he tested extensively on Wimbledon
Common. Sir William's rockets were used by the British military forces both in the Napoleonic Wars and in the 1812 War

against the United States of America, earning a mention in the words of the 'Star Spangled Banner' ("and the rockets' red glare, the bombs bursting in the air, gave proof through the night that our flag was still there".)

## 58. Greenoak Way

Greenoak Way was laid out off Calonne Road in 1982. It is one of those roads in Wimbledon which have been named with local estate agents rather than local historians in mind. The road does indeed boast a couple of splendid old oak trees amongst a smattering of other trees, sufficient to justify its name and the image of verdant tranquillity which that name is designed to create in the eyes of prospective homebuyers.

## 59. Grosvenor Hill

Admiral Drax and his ancestors have dominated recent entries in this book, and this entry continues the saga, for it was a member of the Grosvenor family that was responsible for securing for the Drax family their extensive estates in Wimbledon.

The Old Park estate (also referred to as the Warren estate) consisted of 60 acres, stretching back from Westside to Beverley Brook. It was attached to Westside House which, in conjunction with its neighbour Warren House (now Cannizaro House) had been built in 1705 by a wealthy London merchant, William Browne. After Browne's death, his son sold the estate to Thomas Walker, Surveyor-General of His Majesty's Land Revenue, and on Walker's death the estate passed to his nephew, Stephen Skynner of Walthamstow. Stephen Skynner had two co-heiresses, one of whom, Deborah, married Thomas Grosvenor in 1758. Deborah and Thomas inherited the Old Park estate on Stephen's death in 1765. They had a son called Richard Grosvenor, and in 1788 he married Sarah Frances

Drax, heiress of the Drax family. On the death of their respective fathers the Old Park estate in Wimbledon was combined with the Drax family's extensive estates in Dorset, Yorkshire and elsewhere. Richard changed his surname to Erle-Drax-Grosvenor to reflect the union of the two families. The Grosvenor name was dropped in subsequent generations except for a brief resurrection, as indicated under the entry for Ernle Road, in the very protracted name of the Admiral's mother.

Grosvenor Hill, which first appears in the census for 1865, was named after Thomas Grosvenor. The land on which Grosvenor Hill is laid out was owned by the Drax family, in conjunction with Draxmont which runs off Wimbledon Hill Road just below Grosvenor Hill. Thomas Grosvenor was the second son of Sir Robert Grosvenor (6th Baronet of Eaton) and sat as MP for Chester for 40 years until his death in 1795. This association with Chester may have prompted the naming of nearby Chester House on Westside (and hence Chester Road).

## 60. Hanford Row

This perfectly preserved row of six labourers' cottages off Westside, just to the south of Cannizaro House, was built in approximately 1770 by William Hanford, a London businessman. Surviving records indicate that in 1776 the cottages were occupied by three workmen employed on the nearby Warren estate, a widow, a sawyer and a gardener by the name of Thomas Cannon. When Thomas Cannon moved out some years later his cottage was occupied by John Dorset, previously a coachman at the Wimbledon manor house of Sarah Churchill, Duchess of Marlborough. He was described as "the most sober coachman that I ever saw and very honest and careful of his horses".

*24. Hanford Row, date unknown. (Photograph by I. Munro,
from the collection of The Museum of Wimbledon)*

101

# 61. Haven Close

After the devastation of the Second World War, when over 800 houses in Wimbledon were either destroyed or damaged beyond repair, and the period of austerity that continued for the remainder of the 1940s, the 1950s witnessed a surge in residential development.

Haven Close, laid out in 1959, was one such product of this period of renewed optimism. It was one of three new roads, the others being Castle Way and Beltane Drive, which were created pursuant to the sale in 1957 by the Wimbledon Corporation of 27 housing plots on five acres of land described by the estate agents, Hawes & Co, as the Queensmere Estate. The name Haven Close, no doubt picked with estate agents in mind, reflects its secluded position tucked away off Parkside.

# 62. Haygarth Place

Haygarth Place was developed in 1979 and the name commemorates Wimbledon's best-known cleric, Canon Henry Haygarth, who was rector of St Mary's Church from 1859 to 1902.

Haygarth was educated at Eton and Oxford before embarking upon his life's great adventure, an eight-year sojourn in Australia. Sometime after his return to England Haygarth wrote a book about his experiences entitled "Recollections of Bush Life in Australia", which was published by his Wimbledon parishioner John Murray III (see entry for Newstead Way). Some contemporary Australians might take issue with its opening sentence, written in 1861. "It is now more than ten years since Australia was at the zenith of its prosperity and reputation".

Having sown any wild oats 'down under' Haygarth entered the Church on his return to England, and in 1859 he was appointed rector of St Mary's. Haygarth spent the next 40 years working tirelessly for his Wimbledon parishioners. His most tangible contribution to contemporary Wimbledon was the part that he played in the building of four new churches (Holy Trinity, St John's, St Mark's and All Saints) to cater for Wimbledon's expanding population. He inadvertently contributed to the building of a fifth church, because it was the perceived conservatism of his church services that prompted the evangelical contingent of his congregation to secede and build their own church, Emmanuel, on the Ridgway.

This was a time when Wimbledon's population was growing rapidly, and in addition to his contribution to the spiritual wellbeing of his flock, much of Haygarth's time was devoted to improving their physical condition. Working with the support of local benefactors such as Kezia Peache of Belvedere House, Haygarth waged many campaigns to improve the standard of living of the Village's poor and needy.

It is particularly appropriate that Haygarth Place bears the Reverend's name because he had been instrumental in persuading the 5th Earl Spencer in 1868 to acquire and demolish the slum buildings that occupied the area to the south of the High Street beyond the Dog & Fox, and replace them with "improved workmen's dwellings". These improved dwellings, which were known as Spencer Buildings, were demolished a century later to make way for the buildings of Haygarth Place.

In Haygarth's eyes a key cause of moral turpitude in the parish was the demon drink, and the campaign that Haygarth is best known for was his leadership of the local Temperance Movement. In this capacity he was responsible for the erection of a drinking fountain at the top of Wimbledon Hill Road (which still stands) and for the establishment of a number of coffee houses in the Village, most notably The Welcome opposite the Dog & Fox. The objective of both initiatives was, of course, to deter parishioners from heading to the nearest pub to slake their thirst.

Haygarth died of pneumonia in the vicarage of St Mary's at

the age of 80, and he and his wife are buried in the churchyard of St Mary's.

## 63. Heath Mead

Heath Mead was laid out in 1960 and was another product of the post-war boom in residential development. The Council's minutes of that year indicate that Heath Mead's developer had proposed a different name for the road (not disclosed), which was rejected. The Council's response was to recommend Heath Mead as a name "which is considered more suitable to the locality", and the developer wisely agreed to the Council's proposal.

The Council was correct about the suitability of the name to the locality because Wimbledon Common and Putney Heath jointly represent the largest expanse of heathland in the London area. A heath is an area of open uncultivated land, typically on acid soil, with characteristic vegetation of heather, gorse, and coarse grasses. A mead is an archaic term for a meadow, an area of grassland traditionally mowed to provide hay.

## 64. Heights Close

Heights Close was developed in 1980. Its name reflects its elevated position on the side of Copse Hill, which affords a vista extending to the North Downs.

## 65. High Cedar Drive

Another product of the school of literal street-naming, High Cedar Drive is a near neighbour to Heights Close, and it too has an elevated position on the side of Copse Hill. High Cedar Drive also benefits from the presence of a number of cedar trees, which have survived in what were once the grounds of the finer houses of Copse Hill such as Prospect Place, Holm-hurst and Colebyfield.

High Cedar Drive was developed in 1985 on land belonging to Wimbledon Hospital, which had been sold by the NHS in the previous year for £1 million.

## 66–67. High Street & High Street Mews

The High Street is the only road in Wimbledon Village which has the accolade of being a 'street'. The name comes from the Middle English 'heghe strete', where 'heghe' means chief or principal and 'strete' derives from the Latin word 'strata', meaning paved road (abbreviated from the phrase 'via strata'). The High Street is, of course, the epicentre of the Village, and is almost certainly the oldest road to begin and end within the confines of the Village.

Wimbledon Village was established in Saxon times, and is first mentioned by name (as 'Wunemannedune') in the tenth century will of a Bishop of London. By the time when Sir Thomas Cecil built the first manor house in Wimbledon, in 1588, there were three principal routes leading into the Village; Parkside which led from Putney, Wimbledon Hill Road which led from Merton and the Ridgway which led from Kingston upon Thames. The High Street was the meeting point for all three of these routes.

Until Victorian times the High Street was known as Wimble-don Road. By 1867 that part of the street which runs from the Common to Church Road was being referred to as the High Street, and the continuation of the road from Church Road to the top of Wimbledon Hill Road was known as The Terrace. The latter name was subsequently merged into the High Street.

The Mews behind the High Street first appears by name on the Ordnance Survey map of 1952.

105

*25. High Street, c1875. (Unknown photographer, from the collection of The Museum of Wimbledon)*

# 68. Highbury Road

Highbury Road was laid out in 1907 as part of the development by James Courthope Peache of the Belvedere estate. It was named after Highbury, a district in the North London Borough of Islington with which the Peache family had a close connection.

On the death of James's grandfather, also James Courthope Peache, Belvedere House and its estate had passed jointly to James's only surviving children, the Reverend Alfred Peache (father of the second James) and his sister, Kezia. Alfred and Kezia were both devoted evangelical Christians, and generous benefactors. Kezia, in particular, who lived at Belvedere House while Alfred resided in his allotted parish near Bristol, was a major benefactress in Wimbledon.

The most substantial act of charity conducted jointly by the two siblings was not in Wimbledon, but in North London. In 1863 they donated an initial sum of £35,000 to fund the establishment of the London College of Divinity to provide an evangelical theological education to ordinands who could not go to university. The College (subsequently renamed St John's College) was originally founded in Kilburn, but relocated to Highbury in 1866, and stayed there for nearly 80 years. Alfred and Kezia remained closely associated with the college, in total donating over £100,000 towards its upkeep. At the time of his death in 1900 Alfred was president of the college. It is this long association with Highbury on the part of Alfred and Kezia Peache which was commemorated in the naming of Highbury Road. The college which they founded eventually vacated its Highbury premises during the Second World War, and is now located in Nottingham.

## 69. Hillview

Hillview is the third and final road in an alliterative trio (along with nearby Heights Close and High Cedar Drive) to be endowed with literal names which reflect their position on the side of Copse Hill with extensive views across to the North Downs. Hillview was developed in approximately 1966.

## 70. Holland Avenue

Holland Avenue was developed in 1934, and is named after local dignitary Sir Arthur Holland. Sir Arthur was born in Liverpool in 1842 and, after going to Cambridge University, he joined a Liverpool steamship company, moving to London in 1870 to open a branch office. He subsequently made his fortune by setting up his own steamship and insurance company, Arthur Holland & Co, which developed extensive interests in

South America. In 1874 Sir Arthur, his wife and six children moved into a house called Holmhurst, off Copse Hill.

Sir Arthur played a very considerable part in Wimbledon civic life over the next 50 years. He was Wimbledon's mayor in 1896–7 and again in 1906–7, a justice of the peace and Deputy Lieutenant of Surrey. He was instrumental in the foundation of the Wimbledon Guild in 1907, and was President of Wimbledon Football Club. Sir Arthur was a conspicuous figure in Wimbledon, not least because, as his great-grandson recalls, he took great delight in making local journeys in a carriage pulled by two llamas that he had been sent by a South American business acquaintance. Apparently, the llamas were not particularly popular in Wimbledon because of their habit of spitting at passers-by.

In 1928, on Sir Arthur's death, his wife, Lady Holland, donated part of the grounds of Holmhurst to the Council to become Holland Gardens, named in her husband's memory.

## 71. Home Park Road

Home Park Road lies within the Wimbledon Park House estate acquired by John Augustus Beaumont from the Spencer family in 1846 and developed by him in the 1870s (see the entry for Arthur Road).

Wimbledon Park had been known as Home Park to distinguish it from Old Park on the other side of the Common. Wimbledon Park dates from 1588, when it surrounded the first of Wimbledon's manor houses, Cecil House, and was managed as a deer park to provide meat for the manor. Cecil House was located where Home Park Road runs today, close to the junction with Arthur Road.

The second of Wimbledon's manor houses, Belvedere House, lay outside the confines of Wimbledon Park, but the third and fourth manors were both located back within the Park. In the 1750s, when John Spencer (heir to Sarah

Churchill, Duchess of Marlborough and subsequently the 1st Earl Spencer), was in residence in the third manor house, Marlborough House, he was able to extend Wimbledon Park north to Tibbet's Corner. Some years later in 1764 he commissioned Lancelot 'Capability' Brown to landscape the expanded park, including creating what is now Wimbledon Park Lake.

At the time when John Augustus Beaumont was embarking upon his development programme, there was a very active Temperance Movement in Wimbledon, spearheaded by Wimbledon's rector, Canon Henry Haygarth. Beaumont was a keen supporter of this movement, and wrote into the deeds of all of the plots of land that he sold the provision that "the purchasers shall not exercise or carry on or permit to carry on upon any part of the ground formerly belonging to JA Beaumont a public house or any other building for the sale of wine, spirits or beer". It is for this reason that the Wimbledon Park area remains relatively poorly served for pubs.

## 72. Homefield Road

Homefield Road was developed between 1865 and 1871 and was originally known as Homefield Crescent. It was developed on the site of Home Field, one of the original fields surrounding Wimbledon Village used for grazing cattle. Homefield House was built in 1865. The first occupant was one Samuel Haughton. Under the terms of his 99-year lease he was forbidden from using it as "a lunatic asylum, a blacksmith, a farrier, a leather-dresser, a soap-boiler, or from setting up any steam engine inside".

## 73. Hood Road

Hood Road is another road developed by the Drax family on the Old Park estate. It was laid out in 1937, and, like its near neighbour Barham Road, at the request of Admiral Drax it was named after a ship of the Royal Navy.

HMS Hood was the last battle cruiser to be commissioned by the Royal Navy, and was launched in 1920. She was sunk in May 1941 in the Denmark Strait whilst in pursuit of the German battleship Bismark. Of the 1,418 men on board only three survived. The Bismark was subsequently sunk by other British ships three days later.

HMS Hood was herself named after the 18th century Admiral Samuel Hood (1724–1816). Admiral Hood had a distinguished naval career, seeing active service in both the American Revolutionary War and the French Revolutionary War. He was a mentor to Lord Nelson, who described him as "the greatest sea officer I ever knew". Another claim to fame was that he presided over the court martial of the alleged mutineers on HMS Bounty.

Admiral Drax also had a distinguished naval career. Having served on a number of ships in his early years, he entered the upper echelons of the navy in 1930. In 1939 he led the British contingent in an Anglo-French mission to Moscow which sought to persuade Russia to join the Allies in the war against Germany. Sadly, the mission was unsuccessful. From 1939 to 1941 (when he retired) he served as First and Principal Naval Aide-de-Camp to the King. At some stage in his career he appears to have incurred the displeasure of naval intelligence officer Ian Fleming, who retaliated by naming one of his James Bond villains Hugo Drax.

In addition to his naval career, Admiral Drax was a prolific author. Many of his published works concerned his naval experiences, but he had eclectic interests, publishing for example 'A handbook of Solar Heating'. His last book, published shortly before his death in 1967, was fittingly entitled 'The Uncertain Future'.

## 74. Kinsella Gardens

Kinsella Gardens was developed in 1999 on the edge of the Common off Camp Road. It was built on the site of a 19th century house called Kinellan. The developer's original intention had been to name the road after this house, but this got lost in translation. As the developer subsequently wrote, "We just got the spelling wrong!"

Kinellan was one of those houses that John Samuel Wanley Sawbridge-Erle-Drax, former owner of the Old Park estate, had been able to build before his plans to extensively develop this part of the Common were blocked by denying him and his builder, Mr Dixon, right of access to the Common via Camp Road (see entry for Camp Road).

Between approximately 1884 and 1910 the occupant of Kinellan House was Herbert Fortescue Lawford. Lawford, a stockbroker by profession, was for a while jointly ranked the world's number one tennis player. He won Wimbledon in 1887 and was runner-up on five other occasions. In addition, his stroke, 'the Lawford forehand', is credited with introducing topspin to the game of tennis.

On his retirement in 1910, Lawford moved up to Scotland. It is possible that either Lawford, or his father Thomas Acland Lawford who lived with him at Kinellan, was responsible for naming the house after the picturesque Loch Kinellan in the Scottish Highlands.

## 75. Lake Road

Lake Road was developed on the Wimbledon Park estate acquired by John Augustus Beaumont in 1846. Beaumont developed Lake Road in the 1870s, placing two large pillars at the entrance to the road because this marked the boundary of the estate that he had acquired. He named it Lake Road because it leads in the general direction of Wimbledon Park lake.

## 76. Lampton House Close

Lampton House Close is named after Lampton House, which was built in the Art & Crafts style in 1912. The close was laid out, and further houses built there, in 1955. This development took place at the same time as the development of nearby Deepdale, Margin Drive and Windy Ridge Close.

## 77–80. Lancaster Avenue, Gardens, Place & Road

These roads are named after the Reverend Thomas Lancaster, vicar of St Mary the Virgin in Merton and also a school head-master. In 1789 he purchased the building which is today known as Eagle House on the High Street at a cost of £2,300 to set up an "Academy for Young Noblemen and Gentlemen". He subsequently sold off some of its grounds to help fund the running of the school, and although the Lancaster roads were not laid out until much later they were named in his memory.

The Reverend Lancaster's school soon developed a reputation as one of the leading private schools in London. The school's most famous pupil was the future philosopher Arthur Schopenhauer, who spent three months there in 1803. By all accounts he was deeply unimpressed by the school, the Reverend and his fellow pupils, whom he referred to as "unruly simpletons".

Amongst the Reverend's parishioners in Merton was Lord Nelson. In 1805 Nelson paid a visit to the school, and shortly afterwards the school was renamed Nelson House. Later that year, at the Reverend's request, Nelson took Lancaster's 14–year old son to serve on HMS Victory shortly before the Battle of Trafalgar.

Eagle House is the second oldest building in Wimbledon after the Old Rectory. It was built in approximately 1613 by a London merchant, Robert Bell, who was one of the founders of the East India Company. Just prior to its purchase by

Thomas Lancaster its occupant had been William Grenville, a politician who served under William Pitt the Younger before himself becoming Prime Minister in 1806. The building reputedly acquired its current name when a later headmaster, who had previously run an Eagle House school in Hammersmith, brought with him to Wimbledon an ornamental eagle which continues to sit on the building's central gable.

Lancaster Road, Place and Avenue were developed between 1890 and 1899, and Lancaster Gardens in 1933. Lancaster Place was originally known as Lancaster Cottages, and was renamed Lancaster Place after the Second World War.

## 81. Lauriston Road

Lauriston Road is named after Lauriston House. The house was originally known as Laurel Grove, and was built in 1724 for William Jackson, a glass manufacturer. It was one of a number of fine houses to be built on Southside in the first half of the 18th century, fronting onto the Common with gardens stretching back to the Ridgway.

Laurel Grove's most famous resident was William Wilberforce, who inherited the house in 1777, and who is, of course, known for the leading part that he played in securing the abolition of the slave trade. William Pitt the Younger, who became Britain's youngest-ever Prime Minister in 1783 at the age of 24, frequently visited Wilberforce at Laurel Grove.

The house was renamed Lauriston House in the 1870s and the grounds of the house were sold off for the development of Lauriston Road in the 1890s. Lauriston House was badly damaged in the Second World War, and subsequently demolished in 1958. Sadly, its demolition resulted in the destruction of magnificent allegorical murals which had been painted in the main stairwell, at the commission of William Wilberforce's uncle, by the famous Swiss neoclassical artist Angelica Kaufmann.

# 82. Lawson Close

Lawson Close was developed in 1982 and is named after John Lawson, a wealthy 18th-century lawyer and developer of properties in Wimbledon. The extent of Lawson's building activities is a matter of some debate. Adopting a strategy prescient of the board game Monopoly, Lawson appears to have focused on developing a stronghold of properties at the corner of the Common where Southside meets Westside. He is known to have built Gothic Lodge on Woodhayes Road and is thought to have owned, but not occupied, Chester House. There is some debate over the extent of his involvement in the building of Southside House.

It is known that in 1751 John Lawson took out an insurance policy on "two houses, adjoining, not quite finished". These two houses were known as Holme Lodge and Southside House. What is disputed is whether the two houses were built from scratch, or whether they represented a redevelopment of an existing house. Wimbledon's leading historian, Richard Milward, could find no records of any building on the site of these houses prior to 1751. Others maintain that a Southside House had been built much earlier in 1687 by Robert Pennington, a Chancery clerk, around an older farmhouse, Holme Farm. Under this scenario, the role of John Lawson, who had married into the Pennington family, was restricted to extending the existing house. What is clear from photographic evidence is that the merger of the two adjoining houses to form the current Southside House did not take place until the 20th century.

For someone who undoubtedly played a significant role in the development of Wimbledon Village, very little is known about John Lawson, except that he died in 1764 and is buried in the churchyard of St Mary's.

## 83. Leopold Road

Leopold Road was developed by John Augustus Beaumont on the Wimbledon Park estate in approximately 1872, at about the same time as the adjoining Arthur Road. Like Arthur Road, Leopold Road was patriotically named after one of Queen Victoria's sons.

Prince Leopold, Duke of Albany (1853–84) was Queen Victoria's fourth son. He was named after his great-uncle, King Leopold I of Belgium. Leopold inherited haemophilia from his mother, and died at the early age of 30.

The commercial properties in Leopold Road were established some years after the road was laid out. The shops on the south side were developed in the 1890s, and were originally known as Woodside Parade, and those on the north side were

*26. Leopold Road, c1910. (Photograph reproduced by permission of London Borough of Merton)*

115

developed in the 1900s and were known as Wimbledon Park Parade.

## 84. Lincoln Avenue

Lincoln Avenue was developed in 1961, and was named after Lincoln House, a Parkside house which had been demolished in 1959 to make way for the new development. Lincoln House had been named by its owner, Dr Richard Seligman, after his father Isaac Seligman's house of the same name in the London Borough of Lambeth.

Isaac Seligman was one of eight Jewish brothers who had emigrated from Germany to the USA in the mid-19th century and set up a merchant bank, J & W Seligman & Co. Isaac later moved to the UK to run the London branch of the bank, and named his Lambeth house in honour of Abraham Lincoln.

Isaac's admiration for Abraham Lincoln may well have been prompted by the President's active support for Jewish people at a time of some anti-Semitism in US society. Isaac's eldest brother, Joseph, had been the victim of a high-profile anti-Semitic incident when, despite his status as head of a bank, he had been refused entry to a New York hotel.

Richard Seligman, owner of the Wimbledon Lincoln House, became an internationally renowned metallurgist and successful businessman. He was the inventor of the plate heat exchanger (used in modern combination boilers) and in 1941 persuaded the UK government to adopt his 'high temperature short time' method of pasteurising milk.

Richard was married to Hilda Seligman, a sculptress and leading campaigner against Britain's pre-war appeasement of Hitler and Mussolini. In 1936, Richard and Hilda hosted Emperor Haile Selassie of Ethiopia at Lincoln House when he came to the UK after the Italian invasion of his country. Hilda

made a sculpture of the Emperor which now stands in Cannizaro Park.

Despite the demolition of Lincoln House (54 years after
the demolition of its predecessor in Lambeth), the family's
commemoration of the US president continues, because one of
Richard and Hilda's grandsons, like his grandmother a sculp-
tor, is named Lincoln Seligman.

## 85. Lindisfarne Road

Lindisfarne Road was developed in 1932 and is named after
Lindisfarne House. This house had been built in approximately
1854 by Joseph Burrell, a local solicitor. The house was originally known as St Brelade (named after one of the 12 parishes
of the Bailiwick of Jersey) and was renamed Lindisfarne
House later in the 19th century. It is presumably named after
the Holy Island of the same name off the north-east coast of
England.

In 1883 the house was purchased by Ricardo Modesto
Matias Jimenez, Marquis de la Granja de San Saturnino, a
member of the Spanish aristocracy. The Marquis oversaw the
planting of many exotic trees in the extensive grounds of the
house, several of which are still standing.

Lindisfarne Road backs onto the Oberon playing fields,
which were was once a home farm belonging to Lindisfarne House. In 1931 Sir Harry Twyford, Chairman of George
Brettle & Co, a hosiery company, acquired the land and built
the pavilion as a private sports club for his employees. Sir
Harry was Lord Mayor of London, and lived at Possil House
on Copse Hill (subsequently a nurses' home for Atkinson
Morley's Hospital). The playing fields were named Oberon
after the Company's leading brand of hosiery.

# 86. Lingfield Road

Lingfield Road was laid out in the 1850s, and was the first road to be developed between the Common and the Ridgway. It is named after Lingfield House, which was built on Southside in 1715, although it acquired this name much later.

At the time when the road was developed Lingfield House was owned by the Mansel Phillips family. They had acquired the house, and a number of other properties in the Village, including neighbouring Wimbledon Villa (subsequently The Grange), when Sir Richard Mansel Phillips, MP, had married Caroline Hopkins in 1797. Caroline Hopkins had inherited Lingfield House as part of a portfolio of properties in Wimbledon originally accumulated by her distant ancestor, the banker John 'Vulture' Hopkins. The Mansel Phillips family's property interests included Lingfield Park in Surrey, and Lingfield House in Wimbledon was named after this estate.

Sir Richard Mansel Phillips, MP, was the second son of what the official History of Parliament describes as "an ancient but decaying Welsh family". Richard planned to arrest the decline in his family's fortunes by marrying a wealthy heiress and investing part of her fortune in collieries in the Swansea valley. Unfortunately, neither his business career nor his political career proved to be a great success. He did not help matters by getting involved in a number of scrapes with the law, including accusations that he had obtained money from a constituent under false pretences and had libelled an Irish bishop. His career as an MP came to an end after a fellow Wimbledon resident, Sir Francis Burdett, MP, drew Parliament's attention to his abuse of parliamentary privilege as a means of evading justice.

The decline in the family fortunes continued after Sir Richard's death in 1844, and in the 1880s accumulated debts forced his descendants to sell much of their land and many of their properties, including Lingfield Park (which was to become a racecourse in the following decade), land off Wimbledon Hill Road (which became Mansel Road), Lingfield House and Wimbledon Villa. Lingfield House was subsequently demolished in 1904.

## 87. Lordell Place

Lordell Place was developed in 1995 on the site of what had previously been an accommodation block bolted onto Chester House in 1961 when that building was operating as a training centre for Barclays Bank. Barclays had evacuated their London head office to Chester House at the start of the Second World War, and remained in situ until 1991.

Lordell Place is named after Benjamin Lordell, who is reputed to have become the first occupant of Chester House at the end of the 17th century. Very little is known about Benjamin Lordell, except that he was a wealthy merchant who had trading links with Oporto, in Portugal. He was born in 1655 and died in 1717.

One record that does survive for Lordell is his will. He made his will in Oporto in 1692, being "resolved to embark in a few days for England and not knowing how it may please God to dispose of me". In the main text of the will, he named his brother, Samuel, as his sole heir. As an afterthought he notes that Samuel was to accompany him to England, such that "if it should please God that any misfortune should happen to us both, then I desire that my estate may be equally divided amongst my honoured mother's children". Lordell only made one further addition to his will, in 1713, four years before his death, to bequeath the sum of £30 per annum to one Elizabeth Parsons, who may have been his housekeeper in Wimbledon.

Benjamin Lordell was one of a large and successful merchant family, and one of his brothers, Peter Lordell, was also a Wimbledon resident, and is thought to have built Lingfield House on Southside in 1715.

## 88. Margin Drive

Margin Drive was laid out in 1957, and is named after Margin House, which was itself named after Margin Lake.

In the 18th century the land where Margin Drive runs today was part of the grounds of Wimbledon House. A brief history of this house, which has probably been the most important house in the history of the Village after the four manor houses and the Old Rectory, has been given under the entry for Calonne Road.

In the 1770s the owner of Wimbledon House was Benjamin Bond-Hopkins, who had inherited the estate of the wealthy financier John 'Vulture' Hopkins. At about the same time as Capability Brown was laying out the gardens of nearby Wimbledon Park House, Bond-Hopkins was landscaping the grounds of Wimbledon House. His design included a lake to rival Wimbledon Park Lake, which became known as Margin Lake. The lake was large enough to accommodate an island on which a chapel was built.

In 1900, after the death of Sir Henry Peek, the last owner of Wimbledon House, the house was demolished and the Wimbledon House estate was broken up for residential development. Margin Lake was sold off as part of a plot of land on which Margin House was subsequently built. The first owner of Margin House was Arthur Wills, a barrister and Liberal MP for North Dorset from 1905 to 1910.

During the Second World War Margin House, like its near neighbours Windyridge House and Deepdale, was requisitioned for the war effort. The three houses were not released back to their owners until the early 1950s, by which time they were in such a state of disrepair that the owners decided to sell out to a local builder who consolidated the three houses and their grounds into a 16-acre site for residential development, creating Margin Drive, Windy Ridge Close and Deepdale.

As part of the process of residential development Margin

Lake was drained. Today all that remains of what was once Wimbledon's second-largest lake is a pond in the grounds of Buddhapadipa Temple in nearby Calonne Road.

## 89–90. Marryat Place & Road

Marryat Place and Marryat Road were two of the streets created when the Wimbledon House estate was broken up for residential development in 1900. Like two other streets on the estate (Calonne Road and Peek Crescent) these two roads were named after former owners of Wimbledon House.

Joseph and Charlotte Marryat had lived in Wimbledon House from 1812 until their deaths in 1824 and 1854 respectively. Joseph Marryat's early career was as a merchant, trading with the West Indies. From 1782 to 1788 he was based in Grenada, and he met his American wife, Charlotte, on a trip to the States. He continued his mercantile career on their return to London, and ultimately became chairman of Lloyds insurance market and MP for Sandwich. Marryat, who owned plantations in Grenada, Jamaica and Trinidad, was a vocal opponent of the abolition of the slave trade, petitioning Parliament on this matter in 1807. It was perhaps unfortunate that William Wilberforce, champion of the abolition movement, had vacated nearby Lauriston House some years before the Marryats moved into Wimbledon House.

Charlotte Marryat continued to live in Wimbledon for 30 years after her husband's death, becoming a pillar of the local community and a generous benefactress. She was instrumental in raising funds to build the almshouses in Camp Road in 1838 and to rebuild St Mary's Church in 1843.

The Marryat's children included Captain Frederick Marryat. Captain Marryat had a distinguished naval career, and was responsible for the design of the International Code of Signals and a type of lifeboat. He is best known as the author of many novels, including the enduringly popular 'The Children of the

New Forest'. From 1820 to 1827 Captain Marryat leased Gothic Lodge on Southside for his wife and children. The house bears a blue plaque in his honour, but he can have spent

*27. Charlotte Marryat, c1830. (Engraving by W. Hall after G. Richmond, from the collection of The Museum of Wimbledon)*

very little time in residence as he was on active service in the navy throughout these years.

## 91. Mason's Yard

Mason's Yard was developed off the High Street in 1980, and named after the Mason family, who were long-standing residents of the High Street.

Samuel Mason, a carpenter by trade, was the landlord of The Rose & Crown from 1770 to 1792. It was during Samuel's tenure as landlord that the pub became the starting point for Wimbledon's first public stage coach, the 'Wimbledon Machine' which ran between Wimbledon and Charing Cross. Samuel Mason had the good fortune to marry Mary, the only daughter of Daniel Watney, founding father of the famous brewery family. Mary inherited from her father four cottages that he had acquired on Crooked Billet, where Daniel had lived. In 1782 Samuel used the rents from these cottages and borrowings to buy more land adjacent to the Common on The Green. There were already two houses on The Green, and Samuel built five more, plus some shops, creating an estate from which the Mason family prospered for the next century.

In the 1840s Samuel's grandson Daniel (presumably named in honour of his great-grandfather) continued the family tradition of developing properties on the edge of the Common by building cottages on West Place.

## 92. McKay Road

McKay Road, which was laid out in 1929, is another road on the Old Park estate developed by the Drax family.

It is named after Alexander McKay, who was the Drax family's property agent. The naming in his honour of one of the streets that he helped to develop presumably reflects that

Admiral Drax was happy that McKay had done a good job on behalf of the family.

If the Admiral had had his way, there would have been a great deal more work for Alexander McKay to have done. In 1908 Admiral Drax leased 140 acres of the Old Park to the Royal Wimbledon Golf Club. He subsequently obtained planning permission to develop this land. His plans met with strong local opposition, led by the John Evelyn Society (precursor of the current Wimbledon Society). In 1938 the Society was eventually successful in persuading the Council to purchase the land from the Admiral and to continue the golf club's lease.

## 93. Melville Avenue

Melville Avenue was laid out in 1933 and is named after Henry Dundas, later Viscount Melville, who lived in Warren House (subsequently Cannizaro House) from 1785 to 1806.

Dundas was a close ally of Prime Minister William Pitt the Younger, and also a friend of King George III, both of whom were frequent visitors to Warren House. In the 1790s Dundas was both Secretary of State for the Home Department and War Secretary. During this time Dundas was a vocal and effective opponent of the abolition of the slave trade. It was presumably coincidental that William Wilberforce moved away from Wimbledon the year after Dundas moved in. Dundas's final political appointment was as First Lord of the Admiralty, a post that he held at the time of the Battle of Trafalgar. Soon afterwards his political career ended in ignominy when he became the last minister in English history to be impeached for corruption. He was found innocent, but not long afterwards he retired to Scotland where he died in 1811.

Henry Dundas's wife is also commemorated on maps of Wimbledon Village. In 1793 Dundas had married Lady Jane Hope, daughter of the Earl of Hopetoun, and had celebrated the event by planting Lady Jane Wood which continues to occupy the southern end of Cannizaro Park.

*28. Henry Dundas, 1st Viscount Melville, 1810. (Mezzotint by Edward McInnes, after Sir Thomas Lawrence, published in 1843, © National Portrait Gallery, London)*

# 94. Murray Road

Murray Road was developed in 1907 by the British Land Company in the grounds of Wimbledon Lodge, one of the other great houses of Wimbledon Village. It was named after General Sir Henry Murray, one of the occupants of Wimbledon Lodge.

Wimbledon Lodge had been built on Southside in approximately 1792 for Gerard de Visme, the son of a French Huguenot. Gerard de Visme had been born in London, but had lived for most of his life in Portugal where he made a large fortune as a businessman, possibly importing diamonds from Brazil. He had returned to London with his daughter, Emily, shortly before moving into Wimbledon Lodge. Emily's mother is unknown, and it has been speculated that Gerard had left Portugal with Emily to avoid a scandal. Gerard died in 1797, and is buried in St Mary's churchyard. Wimbledon Lodge passed to Emily, who married General Sir Henry Murray, son of the Earl of Mansfield, in 1810.

General Murray was a distinguished soldier who saw extensive service throughout the Mediterranean during the Napoleonic wars. He is best known for leading the regiment of the 18th Hussars in a brilliant cavalry charge at the Battle of Waterloo in 1815.

General Murray died in 1860 and Emily in 1873. The General is commemorated in a memorial in St Mary's Church. Their daughter, Gertrude Murray, continued to live in Wimbledon Lodge until her death in 1904. Shortly afterwards the house was demolished to make way for Murray Road. Two stone lions that guarded the front entrance to the Lodge were saved, and now stand at the side of the veterinary surgery on the High Street.

## 95. Newstead Way

Newstead Way was developed in the 1960s, and is named after Newstead House which stood on Somerset Road.

Newstead House had been built in the 1850s, and was owned and named by the publisher John Murray III. He chose the name after Newstead Abbey, the ancestral home of Lord Byron, who had been a close friend of Murray's publisher father, John Murray II. It had been John Murray II who, in 1812, had first brought Byron to the public's attention by publishing his great narrative poem 'Childe Harold's Pilgrimage'. John Murray II was subsequently to commit an outrageous act of literary vandalism when, in 1824, in conjunction with Byron's executors, he burnt Byron's memoirs because of fears that their publication would damage Byron's reputation (and perhaps, also, his posthumous book sales).

Newstead Abbey in Nottinghamshire had been an Augustinian priory which was converted to a domestic home after the Dissolution of the Monasteries. It was granted to Sir John Byron of Colwick by Henry VIII in 1540. It remained in the Byron family until 1818 when the impoverished Lord Byron was forced to sell it.

John Murray III achieved publishing success and substantial wealth in his own right by launching in 1836 a series of travel guides known as Murray Handbooks. Their popular success caused Newstead House to be known locally as Handbook Hall.

## 96. North View

The development of North View began in 1882 when two brothers-in-law, Henry Charles Croft and James Erskine Knox, joined forces to build four houses on Camp View and eight houses on what was to become North View. The houses were built on land which had previously been known as Croft's Fields.

Henry Croft was a timber merchant whose timber yard was around the corner from North View on West Place. Traces of the saw pit used by Croft's timber yard can still be found on the edge of the Common opposite West Place.

James Knox was an architectural wood carver by trade who spent some of his later career working on the building of Westminster Cathedral. At the time when North View was developed he lived on what is now Coombe Lane just to the south of the Village. Knox's contribution to the development of North View may have been to put up some or all of the money because, notwithstanding his artisan background, on his death in 1917 he left an estate worth approximately £1 million at current values.

North View was not formally adopted as a public road until

*29. North View, early 20th century. (Postcard published by The Collectors' Publishing Company, London, from the author's collection)*

1894. The name reflects the street's location with a northerly view across the Common.

## 97. Oakfield Road

Oakfield Road was developed in 1929 on the grounds of a house of the same name. The first house on the site had been built in 1852 by John Spriggs Morss Churchill, a publisher of medical books whose company survives today as Churchill Livingstone. Churchill had purchased the plot of land from John Augustus Beaumont, who had himself purchased the entire Wimbledon Park estate from the Spencer family in 1846.

In 1881 the house was purchased by John Frederick Schwann, founder of the London Metal Exchange. Schwann (who changed his family's Germanic surname to Swann in 1917) was a significant local benefactor, co-founding the Wimbledon Hospital and helping to found the Wimbledon Technical Institute (now Merton College). Schwann was related by marriage to the Hospital's other co-founder, Edward Thurstan Holland (see entry for Thurstan Road). Schwann was married to Margaret Anne Holland, who was a cousin to both Edward and Edward's wife, Marianne Gaskell (daughter of the celebrated author Elizabeth Gaskell).

In 1928 the house was acquired by a Miss Amelia Cawthra, the daughter of a Yorkshire industrialist. She demolished the original house and built a new one which she named Oakfield House. In 1929 the Council named Oakfield Road after the house, rejecting an alternative proposal that it be named Park Crest Road. The choice of name reflects the presence of a number of mature oak trees in the area, several of which date back to the 18th century when Capability Brown was employed to landscape the Wimbledon Park estate.

Oakfield House, which had been damaged in the Second World War, was demolished at the end of the 1950s to make way for the development of the Oakfield Estate and Cedar Court.

## 98. Old House Close

Old House Close was named after the 'Old House' which stood at 34 Church Road and which, as the name suggests, was one of the oldest houses in Wimbledon. It was built in approximately 1690 by John Breholt, a Huguenot refugee and London merchant. Sadly, the Old House was demolished at the beginning of the 1960s to make way for Old House Close.

Despite its longevity not much is known about the history of either the Old House or of its first occupant. John Breholt appears to have been a relatively common name at the time when the house was built. One John Breholt was a London shipmaster and entrepreneur, who spent a year in prison in Portugal having been arrested for piracy in the Azores after a failed expedition to Cuba to search for sunken treasure. Much as it would be romantic to claim that the Old House was home to Wimbledon's only bona fide pirate, there is no evidence to prove that the two John Breholts were one and the same.

## 99. Oldfield Road

Oldfield Road was developed at the beginning of the 19th century. It was the first new road to have been laid out in the Village for almost 50 years, and was also the first road to be developed on the south side of the Ridgway.

The land on which the road was developed was originally known as Brick Field. As the name suggests, this field was a source of building materials in medieval Wimbledon. The field was rich in a type of soil known as brickearth, which is suitable for making house bricks without the need to add supplementary materials.

At the start of the 19th century this field was owned by

William Eades, a Wimbledon man who lived on the High Street and owned a grocer's shop. Eades built 15 cottages on Brick Field to be let to local labourers. The cottages were known as Brickfield Cottages and the street was initially known as Brickfield Road.

Later in the 19th century, Brickfield Road became known as Oldfield Road. There is no documented reason for the change, and there are no records to suggest that Brick Field had ever been known as Old Field. Slightly confusingly, there is an Oldfield House located on the adjacent road, Sunnyside.

William Eades was a spirited and controversial member of the local community. In 1818, he took the local Vestry to court over its refusal to reimburse him for expenditure that he had taken it upon himself to incur to extend the workhouse in Camp Road. On another occasion, in 1826, Eades' threatening behaviour towards other Vestry members was brought to the attention of the local constabulary. In 1812, when Sir Richard Mansel Phillips, MP, resident of nearby Lingfield House, was exposed in Parliament for obtaining money from a constituent under false pretences (see entry for Lingfield Road), Hansard records that the money had been used to pay off some of his extensive debts to his local grocer, William Eades.

## 100–102. Parkside, Parkside Avenue & Gardens

In the medieval era Wimbledon boasted only three principal roads, or 'King's Highways'; the Ridgway leading to Kingston upon Thames, Wimbledon Hill Road leading to Merton and Parkside leading to Putney.

The name Parkside was first used in 1893, and alludes to the position of the road bordering the estate belonging to Wimbledon Park House, the fourth manor house which had been built by the 2nd Earl Spencer in 1801, and which was enclosed by a lengthy wall.

As recently as the early 19th century a journey along Parkside was regarded as a hazardous expedition because of the prevalence of highwaymen on the adjoining Common. The most notorious of these was Jerry Abershawe, the so-called 'laughing highwayman', who terrorised travellers along the edge of the Common for many years until he was eventually captured and hanged in 1795, his body being left to rot on a gallows on the Common. Captain Frederick Marryat, author and erstwhile resident of Gothic Lodge on Woodhayes Road, writes of this episode in his novel 'Jacob Faithful'. Parkside ends at Tibbet's Corner which, contrary to popular belief, commemorates not a highwayman but Earl Spencer's gate-keeper, Mr Tibbet, whose lodge was located at the end of Parkside.

Parkside Gardens and Parkside Avenue were laid out in 1903 and 1904, and were part of the development of the Wimbledon House estate initiated in 1898 after the death of Sir Henry Peek, MP, (see following entry for Peek Crescent).

Parkside Avenue was extended at the time of the develop-

*30. Parkside, c1913. (Photograph by Richardson Evans, from the collection of The Museum of Wimbledon)*

ment of Deepdale, Margin Drive and Windy Ridge Close in approximately 1957.

## 103. Peek Crescent

Peek Crescent is named after Sir Henry Peek, MP. Sir Henry was the last owner of Wimbledon House on Parkside. He purchased the house on the death of Charlotte Marryat in 1854 (see entry for Marryat Road). On Sir Henry's death in 1898 the Wimbledon House estate was sold to a development company which demolished the house and laid out a number of new roads on the estate, naming several of them after former residents of Wimbledon House. These roads included Peek Crescent, which was laid out in 1901. The development company had paid £100,000 for the 98-acre estate, which they hoped to sell off at a price of £3,000 per acre, achieving a gross profit of £194,000.

During his time at Wimbledon House Sir Henry made great use of its extensive gardens. He built an array of greenhouses which enabled him, in 1877, to grow the heaviest bunch of bananas, at 97lbs, ever exhibited in the UK, winning him a gold medal at the Royal Horticultural Society Exhibition that year. He also accumulated what was almost certainly the most impressive menagerie ever to have graced the Village. The Wimbledon & Merton Annual of 1905 recorded that, "here was the home of three Indian buffaloes, a Spanish donkey, South American peccaries, a herd of deer, Iceland ponies and sheep, African sheep, emus, parrots of various kinds, Chilean and other swans, geese of every description, piping crows from Australia, pigeons from New Guinea, owls, ducks, wild and tame, and many other curious beast and burden".

Sir Henry deserves to be commemorated with a road in Wimbledon for having played a leading role in the conservation of Wimbledon Common. In 1864 the 5th Earl Spencer, lord of the manor, put forward a plan to enclose Wimbledon

*31. Sir Henry Peek, c1885. (Photogravure by unknown artist, from the collection of The Museum of Wimbledon)*

Common (clearing up the rubbish that had accumulated, draining the swamps and driving off the Gypsies that resided near Caesar's Camp) using funds derived by selling land on Putney Heath to developers. The proposal had many supporters, but met with strong opposition from local dignitaries, including Sir Henry Peek, who led the founding of the Wimbledon Commons Committee. Their cause was subsequently bolstered by the formation of the Commons Preservation Society (led by Baron Eversley – see entry for Eversley Park) and in 1871 they were successful in defeating the Earl's plans. The passing of the Wimbledon and Putney Commons Act in that year preserved the Common in return for the payment to Earl Spencer of an annual rent of £1,200 (which was finally settled in full in 1968).

## 104. Peregrine Way

Peregrine Way is one of four roads in the Village to be named, directly or indirectly, after an animal (along with Almer Road, Beverley Avenue and Sheep Walk Mews).

Peregrine Way was developed in 1977 on the site of a house called Wood Hayes. This house had been built in approximately 1760, and was built to an octagonal design similar to the building now occupied by The Study School on Camp Road.

In 1930 Wood Hayes House and its surrounding grounds were purchased by King's College School, utilising a generous donation from Sir Jeremiah Colman of mustard fame. The school retained much of the land (including the playing field still known as Colman's Field) but the house, which had been damaged in the Second World War and was riddled with dry rot, was sold to developers in 1976.

Why the road was named Peregrine Way is unknown. The peregrine is a wonderful bird, and has the distinction of being the world's fastest living creature (clocked diving at 242mph), but it is not a Wimbledon resident. The 2012 edition of 'The Birds of Wimbledon Common and Putney Heath' by David Wills describes the peregrine as a "scarce airborne visitor" (meaning that it didn't land) seen overhead only twice that year.

It might have been more fitting to have named the road after one of the more notable residents of the former Wood Hayes House. In the 1790s, for example, the house was occupied by Francis Fowke, who had made a fortune in India of at least

£70,000 from trading in diamonds, opium and government contracts. Whilst living in Wood Hayes he commanded the Wimbledon Volunteer Horse Company during the Napoleonic Wars and, more remarkably still, raised 15 illegitimate children with their actress mother, Mary Lowe.

## 105. Preston Road

Preston Road is another road on the Old Park estate developed by the Drax family. It was completed in 1940, making it the last road in the Village to be developed before London bore the brunt of the Blitz. It was to be more than a decade before the next road would be built.

Preston Road was named by Admiral Drax, and the general consensus is that it was named after the parish of Preston in Dorset, which is close to the Drax family's main estate of Charborough House. Preston is a small coastal village, lying just to the east of Weymouth. Preston's greatest claim to fame is that it was home to John Wesley, grandfather of the founder of the Methodist movement of the same name.

The name Preston does also appear in the extended Plunkett-Ernle-Erle-Drax family tree. The great-grandson of Henry Drax and Elizabeth Ernle married an Elizabeth Preston. However, the Preston name does not appear to have survived within the family hierarchy of names, and there is no apparent reason why Admiral Drax would have chosen to commemorate Elizabeth Preston when naming Preston Road.

## 106. Prospect Place

Prospect Place was developed in 1997 in the grounds of a house of the same name that had been built in 1757 by Peter Taylor, a London goldsmith. Taylor named it Prospect Place because it had "an extensive prospect to the south". It was the first house to colonise the land to the south of Copse Hill which had previously been known locally as 'the wild land'.

In 1767 Taylor's son sold the house to Moses Isaac Levy who had made his fortune by securing contracts to provide supplies to the army during the Seven Years' War. In 1771, the house was acquired by James Meyrick, a parliamentary agent, who extensively expanded the estate by acquiring the surrounding lands down to Coombe Lane and across to Pepys Road. Meyrick's acquisitions established Prospect Place as one of the five large landed estates of Wimbledon Village, the subsequent development of which was to shape the Village as we know it today.

After Meyrick's death the house was acquired in 1825 by John Lambton, later Earl of Durham. Lambton was a Whig politician and colonial administrator whose career included a spell as Governor-General of Canada, where he was held in high esteem for being an early advocate of granting parliamentary democracy to the colony. His democratic credentials were not quite so highly regarded in England where he had earned the nickname 'jog-along Jack' for his reply, when asked what constituted a comfortable income for an English gentleman, that "a man might jog along comfortably enough on £40,000 a year" (approximately £3 million in today's money). John Lambton's occupancy of Prospect Place accounts for the naming of Lambton Road and Durham Road just beyond the Village boundary in Raynes Park.

In 1831, Lambton sold the house to fellow Whig politician Charles Pepys, later Earl of Cottenham (see entry for Cottenham Drive, Park Road and Place). After Pepys' death in 1851 the house was sold to the 2nd Duke of Wellington and much of the surrounding estate was sold off to developers. Wellington sold the house itself in 1863 to a Mr Sims who demolished it and sold the site to St George's Hospital to build a convalescent home with a legacy from Mr Atkinson Morley (see entry for Atkinson Close).

## 107–108. Queensmere Close & Road

Queensmere Close and Road are both named after Queens-mere, the nearby lake on Wimbledon Common. The lake is artificial and was created in 1887 (by damming a stream) to commemorate Queen Victoria's Golden Jubilee. It is alleged that the lake was created at the instigation of Queen Victoria herself, who had expressed concern some years earlier that troops attending meetings on the Common of the National Rifle Association had nowhere to bathe. If this anecdote is true, the troops did not have long to benefit from the Queen's inno-vation, because the last meeting of the NRA on the Common took place in 1889.

Queensmere, which is by far the deepest lake on the Common, did become a popular bathing destination for Wimbledon's residents, particularly in the last decade of the

*32. Queensmere Lake, 1923. (Photograph by H.C. Archer, from the collection of The Museum of Wimbledon)*

19th century prior to the opening in 1901 of Wimbledon's Public Baths in Latimer Road.

Queensmere Road was laid out in approximately 1850 by John Augustus Beaumont, shortly after he had acquired the Wimbledon Park estate from Earl Spencer. The road was originally named Durham Road after John Lambton, Earl of Durham (see above entry for Prospect Place), and was renamed Queensmere Road in 1908, some 20 years after the creation of the lake. It is possible that it was renamed to avoid confusion with the Durham Road that existed in Raynes Park.

Queensmere Close was laid out approximately a century later in 1956.

## 109. Rectory Orchard

The Old Rectory, tucked away behind Church Road just north of St Mary's Church, is Wimbledon's oldest building and also its best kept secret. It was built in approximately 1500, and is first referred to as 'Wimbledon Parsonage' in a deed dated 1518. At that time the lordship of Wimbledon was owned by the Archbishop of Canterbury, and the Old Rectory was probably built by Archbishop John Morton. In 1536 one of Morton's successors, Archbishop Thomas Cranmer, was obliged to transfer the lordship of Wimbledon, and with it the Old Rectory, to the Crown during the dissolution of the monasteries.

The house had its finest hour a few years later when, in December 1546, Henry VIII was taken ill on a journey back to London and was compelled to lay up at the Old Rectory to recover. Henry VIII made it back to London, but died the following month. Four years later, in 1550, the Old Rectory was leased as a country retreat by Sir William Cecil, later Lord Burghley, chief minister to Elizabeth I. The Old Rectory was the childhood home of Sir William's son, Sir Thomas Cecil, who in 1576 acquired the lordship of Wimbledon. Twelve years later Sir Thomas was responsible for building the first of Wimbledon's four great manor houses (Cecil House), as a result of which the Old Rectory fell into decline.

The building managed to survive 300 years of neglect on the estate of the lord of the manor. On a map of 1720 it is referred to as "the old laundry house", and during the Spencer era it was used as a dairy house. It was eventually restored by John Augustus Beaumont after he had acquired the Wimbledon Park estate from Earl Spencer in 1846, and was sold by him in 1882. Since that date the house has had a succession of private owners. In 1978 the then owner, Lord Brock of Wimbledon, a leading chest and heart surgeon and one of the pioneers of open-heart surgery, sold off the Old Rectory's orchard for residential development, and Rectory Orchard was formally named in 1981.

*33. The Old Rectory, 1921. (Photograph by G.C. Druce, from the collection of The Museum of Wimbledon)*

140

## 110. Ridgway

The Ridgway can lay claim to being the oldest road in Wimbledon. In the medieval era it linked Wimbledon to its nearest market town, Kingston upon Thames. At least one Wimbledon historian has maintained that it was a Roman road. There are also claims that it follows the route of a Neolithic path linking a farming community based in Kingston upon Thames to the nearest supply of salt, the Thames estuary near Greenwich. There is no archaeological evidence to support either of these claims, but the antiquity of the road is undoubted.

As recently as the middle of the 19th century the Ridgway was a country lane, bordered to the north by the extensive grounds of houses built on Southside, and to the south by fields and meadows running down to Worple Road. A key year in the development of the Ridgway was 1859, when two substantial new buildings were completed, one at each end of the road. One was the Village Club, at the High Street end of the Ridg-

*34. Ridgway, 1913. (Photograph by Norman Jenkins, from the collection of The Museum of Wimbledon)*

141

way, and the other was Wimbledon's second church, Christ Church, at the top of Copse Hill. Both buildings were designed by the same architect, Samuel Teulon, and both were funded by public appeal. Samuel Teulon and the good citizens of Wimbledon completed the transformation of the Ridgway the following year by designing and funding the development of 12 cottages mid-way along the road which soon spawned a small community, including shops and two pubs, the King of Denmark and the Swan.

The name Ridgway (which reflects its route along the ridge of Wimbledon Hill) was in use as early as the Tudor era. The name derives from the Old English 'hryeg weg', meaning road along a ridge.

## 111. Robin Hood Road

Robin Hood Road runs across the Common to Robin Hood Way, close to the Robin Hood Gate entrance into Richmond Park. There is also a Robin Hood Walk in Richmond Park, and there used to be a Robin Hood Farm in the area and also a Robin Hood pub. The use of the name dates back at least to Tudor times and refers, of course, to the legend of the outlaw Robin Hood.

Whether Robin Hood actually existed is unknown. The strongest contender for the source of the legend is one Robert Hood who was referred to as a fugitive from justice at the York Assizes of 1225. Whatever the source, the legend of Robin Hood developed in popular culture over the next century, and the first literary reference to Robin Hood appears in William Langland's 'Piers Plowman' in 1377. Over the next century Robin Hood became firmly established as a folk hero, and by the 16th century Robin Hood had become an established character in the traditional May Games that were held through-out the country.

The area close to Robin Hood Gate appears to have been a

venue for an annual May Games. There is evidence for these games in local church records, which detail income received from the 'Robyn Hoodes Gaderyng' in 1509 and subsequent years. The regular holding of these games appears to be the reason why the name Robin Hood became attached to this area.

Richmond Park was enclosed by Charles I in 1637. Robin Hood Gate was named much later, in approximately 1750, and it is likely that Robin Hood Road acquired its name at about the same time. In the 18th century Caesar's Well on the Common (close to Caesar's Camp) was known as Robin Hood Well.

## 112. Rokeby Place

Rokeby Place, off Copse Hill, was developed in 1982 on the former playing fields of Rokeby School. Rokeby Place is one of two streets in the Village to be named after a school, the other being Beltane Drive.

Rokeby School has been based in Kingston upon Thames since 1966, but was originally located in Wimbledon. The school was founded in 1877 by Charles Daniel Olive, and was initially based in a house at 47 Woodhayes Road and known as 'Helmsley' after that house. It was relocated to 17 The Downs, off the Ridgway, in 1879, two years after its foundation, and became known as Rokeby. There is no definitive explanation for the school's name, but the most likely answer is that the house which the school occupied in The Downs was already called Rokeby.

The house may have been named after Rokeby Park, a country house in County Durham, which was the original English home of Velazquez's celebrated painting 'The Rokeby Venus', and was also the inspiration for Sir Walter Scott's epic 1812 poem 'Rokeby'.

## 113. Royal Close

Royal Close was developed in 1998 on the site of what had previously been Southlands College, a Methodist teacher training college which relocated to Roehampton in the 1990s.

The site had originally been home to Beltane School, which gave its name to the adjacent Beltane Drive. Beltane School had vacated the premises at the start of the Second World War, and the school building had been converted into an internment camp specifically to interrogate captured German scientists. Approximately 250 such prisoners passed through its doors before the camp was relocated to Hampstead in 1947.

The building then remained unused for a number of years until it was acquired by the Methodists in 1961, and renamed Queensmere House because Beltane, which is the name of a pagan Celtic festival, was deemed inappropriate for a Christian organisation. Queensmere House was named after nearby Queensmere Lake (created and named in 1887 to commemorate Queen Victoria's Golden Jubilee).

Following the relocation of Southlands College to Roehampton the site was initially acquired by the All England Lawn Tennis & Croquet Club. The club subsequently sold the buildings and surrounding land to a property developer, who renovated Queensmere House and built six town houses on what is now Royal Close.

The name Royal Close builds on the regal theme inspired by Queensmere House but, as impressive as this building is, the close has no actual connections to royalty.

## 114. Rushmere Place

Rushmere Place was developed in the early 1990s in what was formerly part of the rear garden of Eagle House on the High

Street. The name is taken from nearby Rushmere Pond on the Common.

Rushmere Pond has been known by this name since at least the Tudor era, and is by some way the oldest pond on the Common. In Tudor times the pond was a source of rushes for use as a thatching material and floor covering for huts and cottages in the Village.

## 115. Rydon Mews

Rydon Mews was developed in 2001 on the site of a house at 104 Ridgway which had been built in 1906. This house had been named 'Heorthfest', an Anglo-Saxon word meaning 'men who had a dwelling or hearthstone of their own'.

Heorthfest was the childhood home of Patrick Fawcett, an Anglican priest and professional actor who published 'Memories of a Wimbledon Childhood, 1906–1918' (see bibliography). In this book, Fawcett paints a detailed picture of a Wimbledon that was much less developed than it is today. He recalls, for example, that Heorthfest overlooked a field known as 'Bond's field'(which now houses KCS's swimming pool), which was home to 'Bond's cow', kept to provide fresh milk for Mr Bond's consumptive daughter. He also recalls that the land to the east of his house, at the top of Copse Hill (now home to a tennis club), was at that time the Ladies' Archery Club. Beyond this club, with the exception of Thurstan Road and the Wimbledon Hospital, the land to the right of Copse Hill was dense woodland all the way down to Coombe Lane.

Heorthfest was renamed Rydons many years after Patrick Fawcett and his family had moved on. Lieutenant Colonel HJ Rydon was a former soldier who had retired from the Royal Armoured Corps in 1953 and died in 1958, leaving the residue of his estate to the Worshipful Company of Innholders. The Company used his legacy to acquire Heorthfest for conversion to an elderly care home to be run by the Friends of the Poor.

The home was opened in 1962, and named Rydons in honour of its benefactor.

The care home functioned for approximately 30 years before being closed in the 1990s to make way for Rydon Mews.

## 116. St Aubyn's Avenue

St Aubyn's Avenue was developed between 1932 and 1937 on the site of a house called St Mary's, which had been demolished in 1932.

St Mary's had been the residence of Sir Joseph Bazalgette, who from 1856 to 1888 was chief engineer to London's Metropolitan Board of Works. Sir Joseph's engineering achievements contributed significantly to the health and well-being of the City of London's residents. His greatest achievement was the creation (in response to the "great stink" of 1858) of a sewer network for central London which was instrumental in relieving the city from cholera epidemics, and improving the water quality of the River Thames.

The naming of St Aubyn's Avenue is something of a mystery. Clearly it could not have been called St Mary's after the house because the Village already had a St Mary's Road (see the entry below). Richard Milward, the doyen of Wimbledon local history, believed that it was "almost certainly named after a family which lived in the area between the wars".

The St Aubyn family has a long-established pedigree, and the St Aubyns are best known as having been the custodians of St Michael's Mount in Cornwall since 1647. There was indeed a representative of the family, Arthur St John Knollys St Aubyn, residing in Wimbledon in the 1930s, but there is no obvious reason why he should have had a street named after him.

*35. Sir Joseph Bazalgette, c1877. (Woodbury type photograph by Lock & Whitfield, © National Portrait Gallery, London)*

## 117. St Mary's Road

St Mary's Road has been in existence since at least the middle of the 19th century. The road was originally known as Hot-house Lane because it led down to the kitchen gardens, complete with greenhouses, which were part of Earl Spencer's estate and which were situated approximately where Wimbledon Library is today. In the 19th century the road became known as part of Church Road, and it was only in 1921 that it acquired its current name.

St Mary's Road is named after St Mary's Church. The present church is the fourth church to stand on this site. The first church was built in late Saxon times, and was mentioned in the Domesday Book of 1086 as the church of the manor of Mortlake. The second church was built at the end of the 13th century, and the third church in 1788.

The second church had lasted for some 500 years before it became too small for the Village's burgeoning community. The third church lasted a mere 50 years before it was outgrown by

*36. St Mary's Church, 1809. (Print of the Georgian church, built in 1788 and replaced by the current church in 1843, by and published by S. Woodburn, from the collection of The Museum of Wimbledon)*

148

Wimbledon's rapidly expanding population. The fourth and present church was built in 1843, and was designed by the great Victorian architect Sir George Gilbert Scott in conjunction with his partner, William Moffat. Scott and Moffat were given a budget of only £4,000 to build the new church, which they achieved by utilising as much of the previous building as possible.

The oldest surviving part of the church is the Cecil Chapel, which was built in the 1620s by Sir Edward Cecil, son of Sir Thomas Cecil who had built Wimbledon's first manor house. The Cecil Chapel contains the only piece of medieval stained glass in the church, a 15th-century depiction of St George.

## 118. Seymour Road

Seymour Road was part of the first phase of development conducted by John Augustus Beaumont after he had purchased the Wimbledon Park estate from the 4th Earl Spencer in 1846. The road was laid out in approximately 1850, and was named after the Duke of Somerset, whose family name was Seymour, and who at that time was the sitting tenant in the house that Beaumont had just acquired.

Wimbledon Park House was Wimbledon's fourth and final manor house, and had been built by the 2nd Earl Spencer in 1801, some years after the destruction by fire of the third manor house (the Marlborough house) in 1785.

Earl Spencer, who had got into debt, let Wimbledon Park House to the 11th Duke of Somerset in 1827 for £800 per annum. The Duke continued to rent the house until his death in 1855 and it was not until 1860 that Beaumont was eventually able to occupy the house that he had acquired in 1846.

The Dukedom of Somerset is one of the great peerages of the realm, and the best-known member of the Seymour family is Jane Seymour, third wife to Henry VIII. The 1st Duke of Somerset was Jane's brother, Edward Seymour, who became

Lord Protector of England during the minority of his nephew, Jane's son Edward VI. Edward Seymour was deposed, indicted and executed in 1552, and the dukedom was not restored to the Seymour family until 1588.

The tenant of Wimbledon Park House, the 11th Duke of Somerset, was also an Edward Seymour, but he led a rather more sedate life than his earlier namesake. He was a keen mathematician and scientist, and served as President of the Linnean Society of London and of the Royal Institution. One of his more defining acts was to change his family name from Seymour to its original Norman spelling, St Maur. His descendants retain this name, but the dukedom itself has subsequently passed to another branch of the family which has retained the anglicised version of the surname.

## 119. Sheep Walk Mews

Sheep Walk Mews, which in the 1970s became a small cul-de-sac running off the Ridgway towards the Common, was named to commemorate a medieval path that used to run along the edge of the Lingfield House estate from the Common to the Ridgway. As the name suggests, it used to be a route for villagers to lead their sheep and other livestock from the Common to graze on the fields that extended below the Ridgway.

Although Lingfield Road and its neighbour, The Grange, were only developed in the second half of the 19th century, the Sheep Walk appears to have fallen into disuse much earlier. In 1794, Gerard de Visme, owner of Wimbledon Lodge on Southside, described the walk as "very narrow, incommodious and dangerous for foot passengers".

# 120. Somerset Road

Somerset Road has the same provenance as Seymour Road. It was part of the first phase of development conducted by John Augustus Beaumont after he had purchased the Wimbledon Park estate from the 4th Earl Spencer in 1846. The road was laid out in approximately 1850, and was named after the Duke of Somerset (family name Seymour) who at that time was the occupant of Wimbledon Park House.

Having finally moved into Wimbledon Park House in 1860, John Augustus Beaumont and his family lived there for only 12 years before Beaumont sold the house, but not the surrounding estate, to a Mrs Evans. Beaumont died in 1886, and the Wimbledon Park estate which surrounded the house passed to his daughter. Augusta Beaumont had no attachment to Wimbledon Park, and her plans to drain the lake and sacrifice the park to further residential development were only thwarted when the Wimbledon Council agreed to acquire what was left of Wimbledon Park in 1914.

Wimbledon Park House itself was to remain in private hands until 1948. The final occupants of Wimbledon's last manor house were an exotic couple known as Prince and Princess Wiasemsky. Princess Wiasemsky's maiden name was Rosalie Selfridge, and she was the daughter of Harry Gordon Selfridge, founder of the eponymous department store. Prince Wiasemsky's original name was Serge de Bolotoff. His mother, a Russian émigré, had petitioned the Tzar of Russia for her family's right to use the princely title. The Prince was an early pioneer of aviation, and claimed to be only the fifth person in the world to have flown in a plane. In 1908 the Prince attempted to win a £1,000 reward offered by the Daily Mail for the first aviator to fly the English Channel. His bid failed because the tri-plane that he designed proved to be too heavy to get off the ground.

The Prince may have spent too much money on aeroplanes

and not enough money on his house, which had fallen into an increasing state of disrepair, including widespread dry rot. In 1948, Prince and Princess Wiasemsky were compelled to sell the house to the Council, which concluded that it was beyond repair, and demolished it the following year.

# 121. Southside

Southside, named after its position on the south side of the Common, began life as a pathway linking the Village to the small hamlet that had sprung up at the Crooked Billet around the time of the building of Chester House in 1680. Chester House was the first of a number of fine houses to be built along the west and south sides of the Common. By the middle of the 18th century these houses included Westside House (1705), Warren House (now Cannizaro House, 1705), Lingfield House (1715), Lauriston House (1724), Wimbledon Villa (subsequently The Grange, 1747) and Southside House (1751).

In 1759 the local Vestry (the equivalent of today's local council) responded to this spate of development around the edges of the Common by commissioning the building of two roads, Southside and Westside, to accommodate the horse-drawn carriages used by the owners of these fine houses.

Some indication of the social standing of Southside in the century after the road was laid out is given by the number of members of the peerage who occupied its houses. Residents included the Duke of Newcastle, the Earl of Lucan, Earl Bathurst and the Countess of Bristol. Southside's most noble resident, however, was perhaps the commoner William Wilberforce (see entry for Wilberforce Way).

The most enigmatic of the fine houses mentioned above is undoubtedly Southside House. The origins of the house have been the subject of some debate (see entry for Lawson Close), but what is certain is that Southside House today is a treasure trove of eclectic objets d'art and historical curios accumulated by one family, the Penningtons, and lovingly curated in the second half of the 20th century by the then owner, Major Malcolm Munthe. The Major was himself an enigmatic figure whose life had been transformed by his experiences in the Second World War. Munthe was a member of the Special Operations Executive set up at the start of the war to conduct reconnaissance, espionage and sabotage behind enemy lines. He emerged from the war a hero but also a damaged man, not least as a result of severe head injuries incurred during the Allied landings at Anzio in Italy. After an unsuccessful attempt at launching a political career, Munthe devoted much of his later life to maintaining his family's two UK properties, Hellens Manor in Herefordshire and Southside House in Wimbledon.

It was primarily Munthe who furnished Southside House and its contents with a portfolio of stories involving some of history's most romantic figures, including Anne Boleyn, Marie Antoinette, Lord Byron, Lord Nelson and Emma Hamilton. Whereas many of these stories may well be apocryphal, the Major's own parents both had stories to tell of connections with royalty which were every bit as romantic as some of these other tales.

The Major's mother was Hilda Pennington-Mellor, the daughter of a Victorian businessman who had made a substantial fortune trading between Liverpool and Brazil. It was Hilda who had purchased two semi-detached houses in the 1930s and combined them to form Southside House as we know it today. In her youth, Hilda, whose father's houses included a chateau in Biarritz, had been courted by King Alexander Obrenovic of Serbia. When Hilda subsequently announced her marriage to someone else the King's mother, Queen Natalija, sent Hilda a collection of family heirlooms many of which were to end up at Southside House.

The Major's father, whom Hilda married in preference to the King, was Axel Munthe, a dashing Swede who was the long-standing doctor to Queen Victoria of Sweden. Axel, who was soon to separate from Hilda and their two young sons and live out the rest of his life in Capri, was to write a book of memoirs, 'The Story of San Michele' (his villa in Capri) which unexpectedly became one of the best-selling books of the first half of the 20th century.

Today Southside House is managed by the Pennington-Mellor-Munthe Charity Trust, and is a venue for concerts, lectures, literary evenings and other community-serving activities.

## 122. Steeple Close

The original building in what is now Steeple Close was the vicarage for nearby St Mary's Church, which had been built early in the second half of the 19th century. A road leading to the vicarage had been known as Vicarage Road. The vicarage was converted into residential accommodation and renamed Steeple Court in the 1960s, at which time the existing Steeple Close was laid out.

The name refers to the steeple of St Mary's Church which overlooks the close. The tower and spire of the Church are 196 feet tall, and were designed (as was the church as a whole) by the celebrated architect Sir George Gilbert Scott.

## 123. Strachan Place

Strachan Place comprises eight Victorian cottages adjacent to the Crooked Billet, and is named after Richard and Ann Strachan, who were responsible for their development.

Richard Strachan is described in a neighbour's memoir of the 1850s as "a scenery shifter at theatres, famous for the nuts and filberts which he grew". By the time of the 1861 census he has become a man of somewhat greater substance, describing himself as a "fund-holder". This change in circumstance appears to stem from his inheritance from his father of a cottage and some land. A decade later Richard built three substantial houses on the land, one of which he inscribed "RJS 1874".

Richard died in 1878, and five years later his widow, Ann, demolished their cottage and rebuilt two blocks of smaller cottages on which she placed a plaque, which is still present, inscribed "Strachan Place 1883".

## 124–125. Sunnyside & Sunnyside Place

Sunnyside was developed in the 1850s. The name reflects its position on the slope of Wimbledon Hill, and was clearly chosen to attract potential buyers to the new houses.

A recent review of the 1861 census revealed that the occupants of Sunnyside's nine townhouses included three members of the peerage, a hop merchant and William Blackford, a bootmaker whose shop was nearby on the High Street.

Sunnyside Place is a modern development of townhouses built in 1966 on the site of what had previously been 6 Sunnyside.

## 126. Sunset Road

Sunnyside to the east of Wimbledon Village is suitably complemented by Sunset Road to the west. Sunset Road extends across the Common from Camp Road, and was originally part of Robin Hood Road. It was renamed Sunset Road in the 1970s. The road offers spectacular views of the sun setting over the Common.

## 127. Sycamore Road

Sycamore Road was developed in 1955 at the same time as nearby Beech Close. Like Beech Close it was given an arboreal name to reflect its proximity to Cannizaro Park and Wimbledon Common. The road has been appropriately lined with young sycamore trees, and there is a much larger and older specimen at the end of the road.

The sycamore is a species of maple tree, native to eastern, central and southern Europe, which was introduced to the UK in the Middle Ages. It is a popular tree with city planners because of its tolerance to urban pollution. The species could be forgiven for having something of an identity crisis; its common name derives from the Greek word 'sukomoros', meaning fig-mulberry, which it is not, and its botanical name, 'acer pseudoplatanus', means 'like a plane tree'.

## 128. Thurstan Road

Thurstan Road was developed in the 1870s and was the site of the Wimbledon Hospital.

The street was named after Edward Thurstan Holland, who was a Chancery barrister and a founder of the hospital, becoming its first Honorary Secretary and Treasurer. Edward was married to Marianne Gaskell, daughter of the famous author Elizabeth Gaskell. Marianne was also an active supporter of the hospital, and held the title of Lady Superintendent.

The hospital was opened in 1870, initially with eight beds. In the First World War it served as a military hospital, treating over 500 soldiers. The hospital became part of the NHS in 1948, and by 1965 it had 81 beds. The decision was made to close the hospital in 1983, and the following year it was sold to developers for £1.8m. The developers built the houses of Grange Park Place on the site.

The houses in Thurstan Road were developed by Sir Henry Peek (see entry for Peek Crescent) who, in addition to being MP for Mid Surrey between 1868 and 1884, was a prolific property developer.

## 129. Walham Rise

Walham Rise is a development of townhouses built off Wimbledon Hill Road in 1974. Wimbledon historian, Richard Milward, wrote in the Wimbledon Society Newsletter of February 1992 that the naming of this development was "a puzzle set by modern developers and sanctioned by the Council".

In response to the Newsletter, Milward received a letter explaining that the road had been named after the developers, Walham Construction.

## 130. Walnut Tree Cottages

Walnut Tree Cottages, originally known as Walnut Tree Row, were built in 1836 by John Bishop, a grocer who resided on the High Street. He took out a large loan to build the cottages, and this loan remained unpaid on his death in 1850.

There are no longer any walnut trees in the gardens of Walnut Tree Cottages, but senior residents recall that there used to be. The name walnut comes from the Old English term 'wealh hnutu', meaning foreign nut. It is thought that the tree was introduced to the UK by the Romans.

One of the earliest residents of Walnut Tree Cottages was Wimbledon's first full-time postman, Samuel Syrett. Samuel lived at Number 6 with his wife, nine children and a lodger. He worked as a postman for 21 years, earning an annual wage of £87 5s 10d. He was forced to retire in 1876 at the age of only 47 due to the onset of chronic rheumatism, and was granted a pension of 11s 9d a week in recognition of his "diligence and fidelity". Syrett must have concluded that this would be insufficient to provide for his extensive family, because he promptly embarked upon a new career as a shoemaker.

*37. Walnut Tree Cottages, 1913. (Photograph by H.C. Archer, from the collection of The Museum of Wimbledon)*

## 131. Welford Place

Welford Place is one of only two street names in the Village the origin of which is completely unknown (the other being Alfreton Close). The road was only laid out in 1969 but no record appears to survive of the rationale behind the name. From a historical perspective the late 1960s and early 1970s were a low point in the naming of Wimbledon streets, with several roads being blessed with names that were either bland in the extreme or which bore no apparent links to Wimbledon's past.

The name Welford Place was probably chosen by the road's developer, and may commemorate the village of Welford in Northamptonshire. There is no known connection between Welford and Wimbledon.

Welford Place was developed on the site of three former

158

houses at 143, 145 and 147 Church Road. The grandest of these houses was Cambridge House, which in the 1880s had been home to one of England's leading journalists, WT Stead.

WT Stead, who became editor of the Pall Mall Gazette, was

*38. W.T. Stead, 1912. (Platinum print photograph by E.H. Mills, © National Portrait Gallery, London)*

a pioneer of investigative journalism, and was widely regarded as the leading journalist of his era. His style of 'new journalism' paved the way for the modern tabloid newspaper. He was best known for his campaign in support of a bill (which became known as the Stead Act) to raise the age of sexual consent from 13 to 16. He was also a pacifist and a spiritualist, and was vilified for his opposition to the Boer Wars. His pacifism also earned him a nomination for the Nobel Peace Prize. In 1912 he sailed for New York to attend a peace conference. His ship was the Titanic, and he was drowned when it struck an iceberg and sank. He is commemorated by two identical bronzes, one in Central Park, New York and one on the Victoria Embankment in London, "to the memory of a journalist of worldwide renown".

## 132. West Place

West Place is an extension of Westside, and the name of course reflects its position to the west of the Common.

West Place was developed in the 1760s and 1770s when the 1st Earl Spencer, Lord of the Manor, sold off plots of land on what was then the edge of the Common to John Paterson (a farmer), James Adams (a blacksmith) and John Watney (a baker and farmer, and member of the celebrated Watney brewing family) to enable them to build workers' cottages.

Unlike the grander Westside to its south, which had been laid out some ten years earlier, West Place was until recently very much an area of commercial activity. In addition to bakers and blacksmiths, West Place in the 19th century was home to a timber merchant and saw pit, and to at least two laundries. Traces of the saw pit can still be seen on the edge of the Common opposite West Place. Other cottage industries included the provision of teas to walkers and the storage of clubs for golfers.

## 133. Westside

The history of Westside is similar to the history of Southside. A number of fine houses (most notably Westside House and what is now Cannizaro House), were built along Westside in the first half of the 18th century, some years before there was an established road along that side of the Common.

In 1759, the local Vestry commissioned the building of the roads along both Southside and Westside, the names of course reflecting their respective locations around the edge of the Common.

The turn of the 18th century, shortly after Southside and Westside had been laid out, probably represents Wimbledon's finest hour, at least in terms of its contribution to the making of British history. At that time Wimbledon Village was heaving with eminent politicians, many of them rather more radical than one might expect to meet on the High Street today.

The first politician of this era to live in Wimbledon was the Marquess of Rockingham, who was twice Prime Minister, and who lived on the corner of Church Road from 1771 until his death in 1782. When he died his house was taken over by Charles James Fox, thrice Secretary of State. Another future Prime Minister, Lord Grenville, resided at nearby Eagle House on the High Street from 1787 to 1790. William Wilberforce was resident at Lauriston House (Southside) from 1780 to 1786 (see entry for Wilberforce Way). John Horne Tooke lived at Chester House (Westside) from 1782 to 1812 (see entry for Chester Road), and his disciple Sir Francis Burdett lived at Wimbledon Villa (subsequently The Grange, Southside) from 1801 to 1812 (see entry for Burdett Avenue). Henry Dundas, Viscount Melville, lived at Warren House (subsequently Cannizaro House, Westside) from 1785 to 1805 (see entry for Melville Avenue). When Melville moved out Warren House was rented by Lord Aberdeen, subsequently Prime Minister during the Crimea War. Lastly, Earl Bathurst, President of the

Board of Trade and subsequently Secretary of State for War, rented Wimbledon Lodge (Southside) between approximately 1797 and 1810. With all these politicians clustered around the Common, it is not surprising that William Pitt the Younger (twice Prime Minister from 1783 to 1801 and 1804 to 1806) was a frequent visitor to Wimbledon.

## 134. Wilberforce Way

Wilberforce Way was developed in 1959 off Lauriston Road in the grounds of Lauriston House (formerly known as Laurel Grove), which was once home to William Wilberforce. Fittingly, 1959 was the bicentenary of Wilberforce's birth.

Wilberforce, who was born in Hull, spent two periods of his life in Lauriston House. In 1768, shortly after the death of his father, he was sent by his mother to live in Wimbledon with his childless aunt and uncle. He lived there for four years before his mother, becoming increasingly concerned that he was falling under the influence of his aunt's evangelical religious views, recalled him to Hull. In 1777, Wilberforce inherited Lauriston House on the death of his uncle, and he moved back there some four years later. He remained in Wimbledon until 1786, when his growing parliamentary commitments led him to sell Lauriston House and move to Westminster.

At this early stage of his life Wilberforce was a great socialite, gambler and all-round bon viveur. For him, Wimbledon represented a welcome rural retreat from the temptations of the city. In 1783, he wrote of his life in Wimbledon that "the existence I enjoy here is of a sort quite different from what it is in London. I feel a load off my mind; nor is it in the mighty powers of Mrs Siddons [the leading actress of the age], nor in the yet superior and more exalted gratifications of the House of Commons . . . to compensate me for the loss of good air,

*39. William Wilberforce, 1833. (Watercolour by George Richmond, © National Portrait Gallery, London)*

pleasant walks, and what Milton calls 'each rural sight, each rural sound'".

It was while he was living in Wimbledon that Wilberforce embarked upon a journey of spiritual conversion that led him to renounce his hedonistic ways and, subsequently, to devote himself to the campaign against the slave trade for which he is famous. His activities in this arena resulted in the Slave Trade Act of 1807, abolishing the slave trade within the British Empire (but not slavery itself), and ultimately in the Slavery Abolition Act of 1834. Wilberforce learnt that the passing of this latter act was guaranteed just three days before his death in 1833.

## 135. Wimbledon Hill Road

In the medieval era Wimbledon Hill Road, which linked Wimbledon with Merton, was one of only three 'King's Highways' in Wimbledon, along with Parkside and the Ridgway. Wimbledon Hill Road has the distinction of being the only street in the Village to refer to Wimbledon by name.

The name Wimbledon has gone through many iterations over the centuries. It was first documented in approximately 950 as Wunemannedune, which can be translated as 'hill of a man called Wynnmann'. Subsequent spellings have included Wymmendona, Wymendon, Wimeldon, Wymbyldon and Wimbledon.

Wimbledon Hill Road itself has also had several other names over the centuries. In the reign of Henry VIII it was known as Bishop's Hill, presumably because at that time Wimbledon was part of the manorial estate of Mortlake, owned by the Archbishop of Canterbury.

In 1865, the road appears on an Ordnance Survey map as Wimbledon Lane. The current name was first adopted in the 1890s.

During the Second World War the road nearly experienced

a further name change. In 1943, shortly after the Russians had won the monumental Battle of Stalingrad, a motion was put to the Council proposing that the name of Wimbledon Hill Road be changed to Stalin Avenue in honour of "our brave Soviet ally". Fortunately, with hindsight, the motion was rejected.

*40. Wimbledon Hill Road, c1910. (Unknown photographer, from the collection of The Museum of Wimbledon)*

## 136. Windmill Road

The road which we know today as Windmill Road was laid out in 1845, and is named after the windmill on the Common to which it leads.

Windmill Road only acquired its current name in the 20th century. It had previously been known as Clockhouse Road after Clock House, which was located on what is now Windmill Road, and not on Clockhouse Close which runs behind it. The history of Clock House is given under the entry for Clockhouse Close.

It is probably not coincidental that in the year in which the

*41. The Windmill, c1875. (Photograph by C. Tear, from the
collection of The Museum of Wimbledon)*

road was laid out it was used as the track for an experimental
railway system, designed by William Prosser. The key feature
of Prosser's design was that his train ran on wooden rails using
wheels without flanges, the wheels being kept on the rails by
smaller guide wheels running against the inside faces of the
rails. Presumably the experiment was not a great success
because there are no subsequent records of Prosser's railway
system being used in the UK.

Wimbledon Common's windmill was built in 1817 after
Charles March, a carpenter from Roehampton, had applied to
the 2nd Earl Spencer's manor court for a plot of common land
to erect "a public corn mill for the advantage and convenience
of the neighbourhood". Charles March was granted a 99-year
lease at an annual rent of two shillings. The windmill remained
in operation until 1864 when the incumbent miller, John Marsh
of Kingston upon Thames, was persuaded to sell the lease back

to the 5th Earl Spencer, who was in the process of developing a plan to enclose Wimbledon Common. The Earl's plan was thwarted by the good citizens of Wimbledon (see the entry for Peek Crescent), but the windmill would not operate again, not least because John Marsh insisted on removing its machinery to ensure that it would be unable to compete with the other mills that he operated in Kingston upon Thames.

Having ceased operations in 1864 the windmill was converted into living accommodation. It continued to fulfil this function until 1976 when, after extensive renovations, the first floor of the windmill was converted into a museum. The windmill's greatest claim to fame is perhaps that Lord Baden-Powell, founder of the Scout movement, was living as a guest in the adjacent Mill House when he wrote his seminal book, 'Scouting for Boys', published in 1908.

## 137. Windy Ridge Close

Windy Ridge Close was developed in 1957, in conjunction with the two neighbouring roads, Margin Drive and Deepdale. It was named after the house in the grounds of which it was developed. The story of the development of these three streets is given in more detail under the entry for Margin Drive.

The house which became Windyridge was originally commissioned in 1913, and was to be named Bowerbank after the parish in Cumbria in which its commissioner, Arthur Carr, had been born. Arthur Carr was chairman of the Peek Frean biscuit company which had been founded by the father of Sir Henry Peek, MP, owner of the Wimbledon House estate in the former grounds of which Bowerbank was to be built. Peek Frean's success as a business had been established by Arthur's father, John Carr (see entry for Currie Hill Close) and Arthur had started out as an apprentice in the business in 1872 at a wage of £3 per week.

The designs for Bowerbank's gardens were drawn up by

Gertrude Jekyll, who at that time was England's leading garden designer (see also entry for Cedar Park Gardens). Sadly, the First World War intervened before Bowerbank could be built and its gardens laid out. It was to be 1920 before a house was completed on the site. This house was named Windyridge instead of Bowerbank, it was not occupied by Carr, and it did not incorporate Gertrude Jekyll's garden designs.

The house Windyridge was named after a 1912 novel written by Willie Riley. Riley was a Bradford-born business-man (managing director of the Riley Brothers Optical Lantern Company) and Methodist lay preacher who turned to writing in his forties and published over 30 novels, many of them set in the Yorkshire Dales. Today he is little-known, but 'Windy-ridge', the most popular of his books, sold over half a million copies. It tells the story of a young woman who escapes from London to spend a year in the fictional Yorkshire Dales village of Windyridge (modelled on Hawksworth). For a few years after the publication of the novel, Windyridge became fashion-able as a house name.

Windy Ridge Close is one of two streets in the Village to be named after a novel, the other one being Cranford Close. Coin-cidentally, when 'Windyridge' was first published the novel that it was most frequently compared to was 'Cranford'.

In 1955, Windyridge House was converted into two houses, and the end of its garden was sold off for the development of Windy Ridge Close.

## 138. Wolsey Close

Wolsey Close is a modern development, built in 1982. The close is named after Henry VIII's Lord Chancellor, Thomas Wolsey. The Henry VIII theme is sustained in the names of the houses in the close, which are Wolsey House, Boleyn House, Cleves House and Parr House.

Thomas Wolsey, whose residences included nearby Hampton Court, may have had occasion to pass through Wimbledon, but there is no evidence of any more substantial link between Wolsey and the Village.

Thomas Wolsey fell out of favour with Henry VIII as a result of his failure to secure Henry's divorce from Catherine of Aragon (one of three of Henry's wives not to be commemorated in Wolsey Close). He retreated from Court to the North of England, and died in 1530 after falling ill whilst returning to London to face accusations of treason.

Henry VIII's only documented link with Wimbledon occurred in 1546 when he too was taken ill on a return journey to London, and was put to bed in the Old Rectory in Church Road (see entry for Rectory Orchard). He recovered sufficiently to complete his journey to London, but died the following month.

## 139. Woodhayes Road

Woodhayes Road is one of the Village's oldest roads. The road is marked (although not named) on the oldest detailed map of the Village, which was completed by the French Huguenot cartographer John Rocque in 1745 as part of a wider survey of the whole of London and its environs.

The name Woodhayes derives from the name of the field which used to occupy the area between what is now Woodhayes Road and the Ridgway. This field is first mentioned in a survey of 1617, in which it is called "Warde Hawes", and is recorded as owned by Sir William Walter. The field appears again in a map of 1776. By this time the field has been divided into four separate fields, named on the map as "West Wadhaws, Middle Wadhaws, Footpath Woodhaws and East Woodhaws".

A significant acreage of these four fields has avoided development and survives as the playing fields of King's College School. These fields are bisected by Wright's Alley, and for many years the playing field to the west was known by

*42. Woodhayes Road, c1912. (Postcard published by The
Collectors' Publishing Company, London, from the collection of
The Museum of Wimbledon)*

the KCS community as Middle Woodhaws and that to the east
as Football Woodhaws.

Woodhayes derives from the Old English words 'warde' and
'haw', meaning a 'protected' (as in shepherded) area of
enclosed land. The latter word survives today in hawthorn, a
bush frequently planted as a hedge around fields. In addition
to the four fields, the 1776 map shows a shepherd's gate at the
corner of Woodhayes and the Ridgway.

A brief history of the house named Wood Hayes, which was
built on Woodhayes Road in 1760, is given under the entry for
Peregrine Way.

Woodhayes Road is also home to Gothic Lodge, which was
built in 1763. In the 1820s Gothic Lodge was home to the
celebrated author Captain Frederick Marryat (see entry for
Marryat Place and Road). However, Gothic Lodge's greatest
claim to fame is that it has the distinction of being the first
house in London to have had its own telephone and electric

lighting and heating. This came about because between 1874 and 1913 Gothic Lodge was owned by Sir William Preece, President of the Institute of Civil Engineers. Sir William, who was a pioneer in his own right in the emerging world of wireless telecommunications, was also a colleague and friend of Marconi, who built a transmitter in the back garden of Gothic Lodge to facilitate the installation of its telephone.

## 140. Wool Road

Wool Road is another road on the former Old Park estate owned by the Drax family. It was developed by Admiral Drax in 1928. Like Preston Road, Wool Road was named by the Admiral after a village in Dorset.

The village of Wool lies at an historic bridging point on the River Frome, equidistant between Dorchester and Wareham. The Drax family have owned Woolbridge Manor, located just outside the village, since it was purchased by Henry Drax in 1733. The manor house was immortalised as Wellbridge in Thomas Hardy's 'Tess of the D'Urbervilles', in which it features as the location of Tess's honeymoon. Hardy's corruption of the name was apt because the name Wool derives from the Saxon word 'Wyllon', which means 'well'.

## 141. Wright's Alley

Wright's Alley is a medieval right of way leading from the Common to the Ridgway. It is referred to (though not by name) in a manor court roll of 1492. It is mentioned again in a survey of 1617, where it is described as running through a field known as 'Warde Hawes' (see entry for Woodhayes Road).

The alley became known as Wright's Alley in the 19th century and is named after Robert Wright, who lived in the adjacent Southside House from about 1800 until his death in 1832.

**43. Wright's Alley, 1913. (Photograph by G.C. Druce, from the collection of The Museum of Wimbledon)**

Little is known about Robert Wright, except that there is a monument to him in St Mary's Church in which he is described as the "last male descendant of that branch of an ancient family, formerly long possessing Santon Downham in Suffolk". He is also described as "esteemed and respected by all who knew his worth, while his pious resignation under the infirmities of increasing years was a blessed example to those who witnessed it".

Robert and his wife, Lucy, had two daughters, both of whom are also commemorated on monuments in St Mary's. One of them, Frances Lucy Wright, died unmarried. The other, Marianne Wright, married Lieutenant-Colonel Clement Archer, and had three children. Her daughter, Marianne Lucy Archer, who had married the Honourable Walter Wrottesley, sadly died in 1848, nine days after giving birth to her second child. She is the last of Robert Wright's descendants to be the subject of a memorial tablet in the Church. The alley named after her grandfather is the last entry in this alphabetical list of the street names of Wimbledon Village.

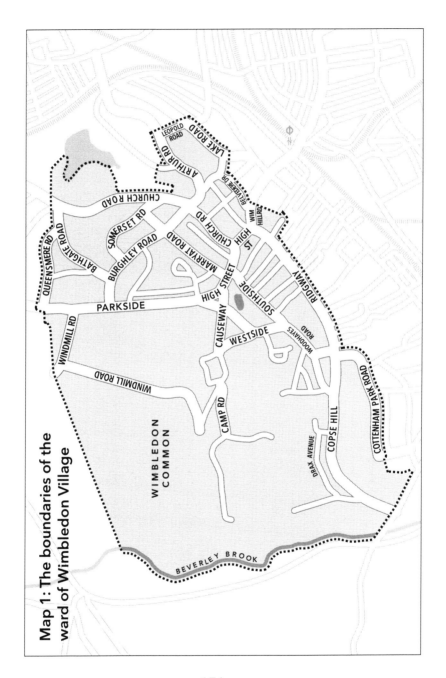

Map 1: The boundaries of the ward of Wimbledon Village

LEOPOLD ROAD
LAKE ROAD
ARTHUR RD
BELVEDERE DR
CHURCH ROAD
SOMERSET RD
CHURCH RD
WIM
HILLRD
BATHGATE ROAD
QUEENSMERE RD
BURGHLEY ROAD
MARRYAT ROAD
HIGH ST
PARKSIDE
HIGH STREET
CAUSEWAY
SOUTHSIDE
RIDGWAY
WINDMILL RD
WESTSIDE
WOODHAYES
ROAD
WINDMILL ROAD
CAMP RD
COTTENHAM PARK ROAD
WIMBLEDON
COMMON
DRAX AVENUE
COPSE HILL

BEVERLEY BROOK

174

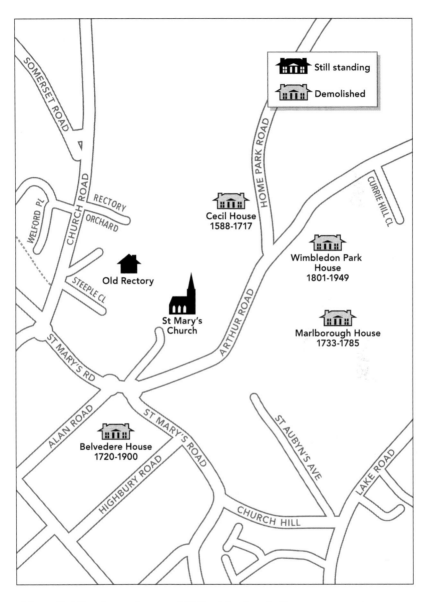

**Map 2: The locations of Wimbledon's four manor houses**

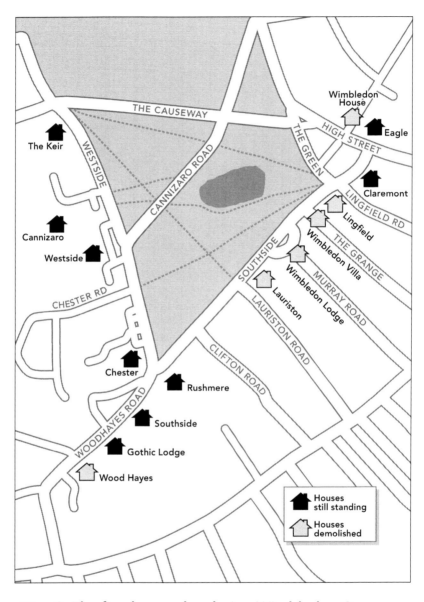

**Map 3: The fine houses bordering Wimbledon Common**

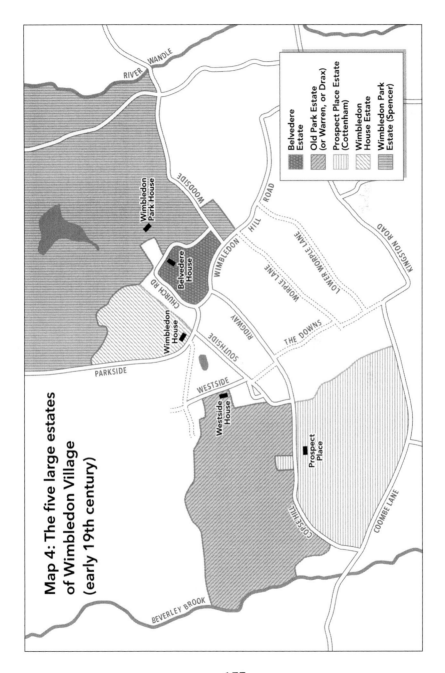

Map 4: The five large estates of Wimbledon Village (early 19th century)

Legend:
- Belvedere Estate
- Old Park Estate (or Warren, or Drax)
- Prospect Place Estate (Cottenham)
- Wimbledon House Estate
- Wimbledon Park Estate (Spencer)

RIVER WANDLE

Wimbledon Park House

WOODSIDE

Belvedere House

WIMBLEDON HILL ROAD

WORPLE LANE

LOWER WORPLE LANE

KINGSTON ROAD

CHURCH RD

Wimbledon House

RIDGWAY

THE DOWNS

PARKSIDE

SOUTHSIDE

WESTSIDE

Westside House

Prospect Place

CORSE HILL

COOMBE LANE

BEVERLEY BROOK

# Appendix 1

# WIMBLEDON VILLAGE TIMELINE (1500–2000)

(Note that some of the earlier dates, particularly building construction dates, should be regarded as approximate)

## 1500–1549

1500   John Morton, Archbishop of Canterbury, builds the Old Rectory

1536   Thomas Cranmer, Archbishop of Canterbury, cedes manor of Wimbledon to Henry VIII, who passes it to Thomas Cromwell

1540   The manor passes back to the Crown on Cromwell's death

1543   Henry VIII grants the manor to his sixth wife, Catherine Parr

1546   Henry VIII is taken ill whilst travelling back to London and stays in the Old Rectory

1548   On Catherine's death the manor reverts to the Crown

## 1550–1599

1550   The Old Rectory is leased by Sir William Cecil

1576   Elizabeth I grants the manor to Sir Christopher Hatton, who sells it on to Sir Thomas Cecil

1588   Sir Thomas Cecil builds the first manor house (Cecil House)
1599   Elizabeth I visits Cecil House

## 1600–1659

1613   Robert Bell builds Eagle House, High Street
1616   James I visits Cecil House
1617   First reference to Wimbledon's oldest pub, the Sign of My Lord's Arms (now the Dog & Fox)
1623   Sir Thomas Cecil dies and Cecil House passes to his son, Edward Cecil, 1st Viscount Wimbledon
1628   Cecil House damaged in an explosion when maids mistook a barrel of gunpowder for soap
1638   Edward Cecil dies, and Cecil House is sold to Charles I for his wife, Queen Henrietta Maria
1639   Inigo Jones employed by the Queen to modernise Cecil House
1649   After the Civil War Cecil House passes to Cromwellian General Sir John Lambert

## 1650–1699

1650   Thomas Hilliard builds Claremont House, High Street. The Sign of the Rose pub opens for business (now the Rose & Crown)
1661   On the Restoration Cecil House reverts to Henrietta Maria (Queen Mother), who sells it
1680   Benjamin Lordell builds Chester House, Westside
1690   John Breholt builds the Old House, Church Road

## 1700–1749

1705   William Browne builds Westside House and Warren House (now Cannizaro House)

1710 Sir Theodore Janssen builds Wimbledon House, Parkside

1715 Peter Lordell builds Lingfield House, Southside

1717 Sir Theodore Janssen purchases Cecil House, and demolishes it

1720 Sir Theodore Jannsen builds the second manor house (subsequently Belvedere House)

1723 Jannsen ruined by South Sea Company, sells the manor to Sarah Churchill, Duchess of Marlborough

1724 William Jackson builds Laurel Grove (subsequently Lauriston House), Southside

1733 The Duchess of Marlborough builds the third manor house (Marlborough House)

1744 Manor passes to the Duchess's heir, John Spencer, subsequently 1st Earl Spencer

1745 First reference to the Crooked Billet pub

1747 Thomas Lewis builds Wimbledon Villa (subsequently The Grange), Southside

1749 Earl Spencer sells Belvedere House to Martha Rush

## 1750–1799

1751 John Lawson builds Southside House, Southside

1752 Workhouse built on Camp Road

1757 Peter Taylor builds Prospect Place on Copse Hill

1758 Wimbledon Free School built on Camp Road (now The Study School)

1760 John Cooksey builds Wood Hayes (Octagon House), Woodhayes Road

1763 John Manship builds Gothic Lodge, Woodhayes Road

1768 Capability Brown designs grounds of Marlborough House (including what is now Wimbledon Park Lake)

1771 Marquess of Rockingham moves into a house on Church Road

1777 William Wilberforce inherits Lauriston House

1780   The first public stage coach, the Wimbledon Machine, runs from the Rose & Crown to Charing Cross

1782   John Horne Tooke moves into Chester House. Samuel Mason acquires and develops The Green

1785   Marlborough House burns down. Henry Dundas, Viscount Melville, moves into Warren House.

1787   Lord Grenville moves into Eagle House

1788   Third St Mary's Church built. John Watney builds Rushmere House, Southside

1789   Thomas Lancaster establishes a school in Eagle House. Abraham Aguilar builds The Keir, Westside

1791   Charles Alexandre, Vicomte de Calonne buys Wimbledon House, Parkside

1792   Gerard de Visme builds Wimbledon Lodge, Southside

1798   2nd Earl Spencer builds the Well House, Arthur Road

## 1800–1849

1801   2nd Earl Spencer builds fourth and final manor house (Wimbledon Park House). Sir Francis Burdett moves into Wimbledon Villa, Southside Common

1803   Lord Nelson visits Eagle House School (subsequently renamed Nelson House School)

1805   Lord Aberdeen moves into Warren House

1817   The future Duke and Duchess of Cannizaro lease Warren House (now Cannizaro House). Charles March builds the Windmill

1825   John Lambton, Earl of Durham, acquires Prospect Place

1827   Wimbledon Park House leased by Duke of Somerset. Drax family inherit the Old Park estate, including Warren (Cannizaro) and Westside Houses

1831   Charles Pepys, Earl of Cottenham, buys Prospect Place from John Lambton, Earl of Durham

1832    First reference to what became the Fox & Grapes pub (originally the Union Beershop)

1834    Belvedere House sold by Rush family to James Courthope Peache. Workhouse on Camp Road decommissioned

1838    Wimbledon Station opens. Almshouses built on Camp Road. Queen Victoria visits Wimbledon Park House

1840    High Street Easter Fairs terminated (at the instigation of Mrs Marryat)

1843    Fourth and final St Mary's Church built by Sir George Gilbert Scott

1846    4th Earl Spencer sells Wimbledon Park House (but not the manorial title) to developer John Augustus Beaumont

1847    Beaumont commences first phase of development of Wimbledon Park estate

## 1850–1899

1851    Development of Prospect Place estate begins after death of Charles Pepys

1854    Sir Henry Peek moves into Wimbledon House, Parkside

1855    The Swan pub opens on the Ridgway

1859    Christ Church built at the top of Copse Hill. Canon Henry Haygarth becomes rector of St Mary's. Village Club opens on the Ridgway

1860    Somerset vacates & Beaumont occupies Wimbledon Park House. First National Rifle Association ('NRA') meeting on the Common

1863    Prospect Place House, Copse Hill, demolished

1864    5th Earl Spencer presents a Bill to Parliament to enclose the Common

1865    Baron Eversley founds The Commons Preservation

Society. Foundation of the Royal Wimbledon Golf Club

1866 Local Board of Health established in the Village, and gradually takes over from the Vestry

1867 The Hand in Hand pub opens

1868 All England Croquet Club established in a field off Worple Road

1869 Atkinson Morley's Convalescent Hospital opened (on site of Prospect Place)

1870 Wimbledon Hospital opens in Thurstan Road

1871 Wimbledon and Putney Commons Act saves the Common from enclosure. Raynes Park Station opens

1872 Beaumont sells Wimbledon Park House and commences second phase of development of Wimbledon Park estate

1875 John Sawbridge-Erle-Drax and his builder, Mr Dixon, destroy the ramparts of Caesar's Camp

1877 Spencer Gore wins first open tennis championship. Rokeby School (originally 'Helmsley') founded on Woodhayes Road

1878 Local Board of Health relocates to the Broadway, into offices which become Wimbledon's first town hall

1885 Wimbledon becomes a parliamentary constituency, getting its own MP, under the Redistribution of Seats Act. Vestry disbanded

1887 Queensmere Lake created to commemorate Queen Victoria's golden jubilee. Wimbledon Villa, Southside, demolished. Wimbledon public library opens

1888 Emmanuel Church built on Ridgway

1889 Final NRA meeting on the Common. Wimbledon Park tube station opened. District line extended to Wimbledon. Formation of Old Centrals football team (forerunners to Wimbledon FC) playing on the Common

1891 Kaiser Wilhelm II, German Emperor, attends a review of troops on the Common

1893 The Study School founded on the High Street
1895 Urban District Council takes over responsibility for local government, replacing the Local Board of Health
1897 King's College School moves from The Strand in London to Southside

## 1900–1949

1900 Belvedere House demolished. Wimbledon House demolished. Cannizaro House destroyed by fire
1901 Beginning of development of Belvedere estate and Wimbledon House estate
1903 Foundation of the John Evelyn Club (now The Wimbledon Society)
1904 Lingfield House, Southside, demolished. Wimbledon Fire Station moved from the Village to the Town
1905 Charter Day. Wimbledon becomes a borough with its own mayor. Wimbledon Lodge, Southside, demolished
1907 Drax family lease part of the Old Park to Royal Wimbledon Golf Club
1914 Council buys Wimbledon Park off John Augustus Beaumont's daughter, Augusta
1916 Museum of Wimbledon opens in the Village Club
1921 War memorial erected on the edge of the Common
1922 All England Lawn Tennis & Croquet Club moves from Worple Road to its current home on Church Road
1924 Admiral Sir Reginald Plunkett-Ernle-Erle-Drax begins development of Old Park estate
1938 Wimbledon Borough Council buys part of the Old Park off Drax and grants Royal Wimbledon Golf Club a 60 year lease
1948 Wimbledon Borough Council buys Cannizaro House, and opens the park to the public in 1949
1949 Wimbledon Park House demolished

## 1950–1999

1965   Wimbledon becomes part of the London Borough of Merton

1976   Buddhapadipa Temple moves from Richmond to Wimbledon (Calonne Road)

1982   John Evelyn Club changes its name to the Wimbledon Society

1983   Wimbledon Hospital on Thurstan Road closes. Parkside Hospital opens.

1996   9th Earl Spencer sells the Lordship of the Manor of Wimbledon to an undisclosed buyer based in Brazil

Appendix 2

# LIST OF STREETS BY DATE OF DEVELOPMENT

**Pre 1750**
Camp Road
Church Road
Dairy Walk
The Green
High Street
Parkside
Ridgway
Robin Hood Road
Wimbledon Hill Road
Woodhayes Road
Wright's Alley

**1750–1775**
Cannizaro Road
The Causeway
Crooked Billet
Hanford Row
Southside
West Place
Westside

**1775–1800**
None

**1800–1825**
Oldfield Road

**1825–1850**
Allington Close
Copse Hill
Walnut Tree Cottages
Windmill Road

**1850–1860**
Cottenham Park Road
Lingfield Road
Queensmere Road
St Mary's Road
Seymour Road
Somerset Road
Sunnyside

**1860–1870**
Belvedere Square
Glencairn Road
Grosvenor Hill
Homefield Road

## 1870–1880
Arthur Road
Bathgate Road
Courthope Road
Home Park Road
Lake Road
Leopold Road
Thurstan Road

## 1880–1890
Camp View
Clifton Road
The Grange
Strachan Place

## 1890–1900
Church Hill
Lancaster Avenue
Lancaster Place
Lancaster Road
Lauriston Road
North View

## 1900–1910
Alan Road
Belvedere Avenue
Belvedere Drive
Belvedere Grove
Burghley Road
Calonne Road
Clement Road
Highbury Road
Marryat Place
Marryat Road
Murray Road

Parkside Avenue
Parkside Gardens
Peek Crescent

## 1910–1920
None

## 1920–1930
Almer Road
Barham Road
Drax Avenue
Dunstall Road
Ellerton Road
Ernle Road
McKay Road
Oakfield Road
Wool Road

## 1930–1940
Atherton Drive
Beverley Avenue
Burdett Avenue
Holland Avenue
Hood Road
Lancaster Gardens
Lindisfarne Road
Melville Avenue
St Aubyn's Avenue

## 1940–1950
Preston Road

## 1950–1960
Beech Close
Beltane Drive

Castle Way
Chester Road
Currie Hill Close
Deepdale
Haven Close
High Street Mews
Lampton House Close
Margin Drive
Queensmere Close
Sycamore Road
Wilberforce Way
Windy Ridge Close

## 1960–1970
Carnegie Place
Castle Close
Cedar Court
Coach House Lane
Cottenham Drive
Cottenham Place
Cranford Close
Heath Mead
Hillview
Lincoln Avenue
Newstead Way
Old House Close
Steeple Close
Sunnyside Place
Welford Place

## 1970–1980
Alfreton Close
Draxmont

Gibbard Mews
Haygarth Place
Peregrine Way
Sheep Walk Mews
Sunset Road
Walham Rise

## 1980–1990
Cedarland Terrace
Clockhouse Close
Eversley Park
Grange Park Place
Greenoak Way
Heights Close
High Cedar Drive
Lawson Close
Mason's Yard
Rectory Orchard
Rokeby Place
Wolsey Close

## 1990–2000
Kinsella Gardens
Lordell Place
Prospect Place
Royal Close
Rushmere Place

## 2000–Present
Atkinson Close
Cedar Park Gardens
Rydon Mews

# Appendix 3
# THE FINE HOUSES OF
# WIMBLEDON VILLAGE

| House name | Location | First Owner | Date built | | Date demolished |
|---|---|---|---|---|---|
| Old Rectory | Church Road | John Morton, Archbishop of Canterbury? | 1500 | to | Present |
| Cecil House (first manor house) | Home Park Road | Sir Thomas Cecil, Earl of Exeter | 1588 | to | 1717 |
| Eagle House | High Street | Robert Bell | 1613 | to | Present |
| Claremont House | High Street | Thomas Hilliard | 1650 | to | Present |
| Chester House | Westside | Benjamin Lordell? | 1680 | to | Present |
| The Old House | Church Road | John Breholt | 1690 | to | 1960 |
| Westside House | Westside | William Browne | 1705 | to | Present |
| Cannizaro House (formerly Warren House) | Westside | William Browne | 1705 | to | Present |
| Wimbledon House | Parkside | Sir Theodore Janssen | 1710 | to | 1900 |
| Lingfield House | Southside | Peter Lordell | 1715 | to | 1904 |

| House name | Location | First Owner | Date built | | Date demolished |
|---|---|---|---|---|---|
| Belvedere House (second manor house) | Alan Road | Sir Theodore Janssen | 1720 | to | 1900 |
| Lauriston House (formerly Laurel Grove) | Southside | William Jackson | 1724 | to | 1958 |
| Marlborough House (third manor house) | Arthur Road | Sarah Churchill, Duchess of Marlborough | 1733 | to | 1785 |
| Wimbledon Villa (subsequently The Grange) | Southside | Thomas Lewis | 1747 | to | 1887 |
| Southside House | Southside | John Lawson | 1751 | to | Present |
| Prospect Place | Copse Hill | Peter Taylor | 1757 | to | 1863 |
| Wood Hayes (The Octagon House) | Woodhayes Road | John Cooksey | 1760 | to | 1976 |
| Gothic Lodge | Woodhayes Road | John Manship | 1763 | to | Present |
| Rushmere | Southside | John Watney | 1788 | to | Present |
| The Keir | Westside | Abraham Aguilar | 1789 | to | Present |
| Wimbledon Lodge | Southside | Gerard de Visme | 1792 | to | 1905 |
| Wimbledon Park House (fourth manor house) | Arthur Road | George, 2nd Earl Spencer | 1801 | to | 1949 |

# BIBLIOGRAPHY

| | | |
|---|---|---|
| Arnold C T | Wimbledon National Schools | 1912 |
| Bartlett, Rev William | The History & Antiquities of the Parish of Wimbledon, Surrey | 1865 |
| Boas Guy, Cloake C S & Warren H J | Wimbledon has a History | 1947 |
| Cranch, Graeme & Miles, Frank | King's College School | 1979 |
| Cooke A A | Old Wimbledon | 1927 |
| Curry, Constance | Memories of my Side of the Common | 1988 |
| Fawcett, Patrick | Memories of a Wimbledon Childhood 1906–1918 | 1981 |
| Gould, Terry & Uttley, David | A History of the Atkinson Morley's Hospital 1869–1995 | 1996 |
| Hall S C | Wimbledon: Illustrative Details Concerning the Parish | 2010 |
| Harvey, John | A Firm Foundation – The Story of the Old Central/Bishop Gilpin School | 2008 |
| Hawtin, Gillian | Battle for the Green | 1993 |
| Hawtin, Gillian | Early Radical Wimbledon | 1993 |
| Hawtin, Gillian | New View of Old Wimbledon (four volumes) | 1993 |
| Hawtin, Gillian | Off to School | 1994 |
| Hawtin, Gillian | Onward Christian Soldiers | 1993 |
| Hawtin, Gillian | Wimbledon | 1994 |
| Higham, C S S | Wimbledon Manor House under the Cecils | 1962 |
| Loobey, Patrick & Every, Keith | Wimbledon in Old Photographs | 1995 |
| Lyson | History of Wimbledon | 1792 |
| Matthews, Tony | Heritage Tales, 52 Stories of Wimbledon | 2013 |

| Matthews, Tony | Cannizaro, Beyond the Gates | 2010 |
| Matthews, Tony | Chester House Wimbledon, Atmosphere of a Past Age | 2014 |
| Mills, A D | A Dictionary of London Place Names | 2010 |
| Milward, Richard | Wimbledon – a Pictorial History | 1994 |
| Milward, Richard | A New Short History of Wimbledon | 1989 |
| Milward, Richard | Historic Wimbledon: From Caesar's Camp to Centre Court | 1989 |
| Milward, Richard | Cannizaro House and its Park | 1991 |
| Milward, Richard | The Rectory: Wimbledon's Oldest House | 1990 |
| Milward, Richard | A Parish Church Since Domesday: St Mary's Wimbledon | 1993 |
| Milward, Richard | Wimbledon Past | 1998 |
| Milward, Richard | Wimbledon Then & Now | 1995 |
| Milward, Richard | The Spencers in Wimbledon, 1744–1994 | 1996 |
| Milward, Richard | Eagle House: a Short History | 2001 |
| Milward, Richard | Wimbledon in the Time of the Civil War | 1976 |
| Milward, Richard | Portrait of a Parish: Jesuits in Wimbledon | 1977 |
| Milward, Richard | Two Wimbledon Roads: the Story of Edge Hill & Darlaston Road | 1991 |
| Milward, Richard | Early & Medieval Wimbledon | 1983 |
| Milward, Richard | Wimbledon's Manor Houses | 1982 |
| Milward, Richard | A Georgian Village, Wimbledon 1724–1765 | 1986 |
| Milward, Richard | Portrait of a Church: The Sacred Heart, Wimbledon 1887–1987 | 1987 |
| Milward, Richard | Wimbledon 1865–1965 | 2005 |
| Milward, Richard | The Wimbledon Society 1902–2003 | 2003 |
| Milward, Richard | Wimbledon Two Hundred Years Ago | 1996 |
| Milward, Richard | Tudor Wimbledon | 1972 |
| Milward, Richard & Maidment, Cyril | The Lull before the Storm: the Last Years of Rural Wimbledon | 2002 |
| Milward, Richard & Maidment, Cyril | Wimbledon, a Surrey Village in Maps | 2000 |

| Myson, William & Berry J G | Cannizaro House Wimbledon & its Park | 1972 |
|---|---|---|
| Norman-Smith, D & B | The Grange | 1984 |
| Parsloe, Guy | Wimbledon Village Club and Lecture Hall 1858–1958, a Centenary Record | 1958 |
| Plastow, Norman | A History of Wimbledon & Putney Commons | 1986 |
| Plastow, Norman | The Wimbledon Windmill | 1977 |
| Plastow, Norman | Safe as Houses, Wimbledon at War 1939–1945 | 1972 |
| Riggs, Charlotte & Cook, Brenda | The History of Ricards Lodge | 1975 |
| Rondeau, Bernard | Wimbledon Park: From Private Park to Residential Suburb | 1995 |
| Veale, Dr Elspeth | Wimbledon's Belvedere Estate | 2012 |
| Whichelow, Clive | Pubs of Wimbledon Village | 1998 |
| Whichelow, Clive | Secrets of Wimbledon Common & Putney Heath | 2000 |
| Whichelow, Clive | The Local Mystery of Robin Hood | 2000 |
| Whitehead, Winifred | Wimbledon 1885–1965 | 1965 |

# INDEX

**Street sub-sections are in bold and illustrations are in italics**

195

196

Grove   25, 27, 66, 67, 95, 113,
   121, 152, 161, 162, 181, 191
Lauriston Road   113, 162
Lawford, Herbert Fortescue   111
Lawson Close   114, 152
Lawson, John   114, 181, 191
Leopold Road   9, 49, *115*
Leopold, Duke of Albany   11, 115
Levy, Moses Isaac   137
Lewis, Thomas   95, 181, 191
Lincoln Avenue   68, **116**
Lincoln House   68, 116
Lincoln, Abraham   11, 116
Lindisfarne House   117
Lindisfarne Road   12, **117**
Lingfield House   25, 95, 118, 119,
   131, 150, 152, 181, 185, 190
Lingfield Park, Surrey   118
Lingfield Road   33, **118**, 131, 150
Little Common Garden   97
Llewelyn, John Dillwyn   50
Local Board of Health   34, 184,
   185
London College of Divinity, later
   St John's College   107
Lordell Place   **119**
Lordell, Benjamin   24, 71, 119,
   180, 190
Lordell, Peter   119, 181, 190
Lucan, Earl of   152
Lukey, THV   50

Mansel Phillips, Caroline, née
   Hopkins   95, 118
Mansel Phillips, Sir Richard   95,
   118, 131
Mansel Road   119
Mansel, Sir Richard   95, 96
Manship, John   181, 191
March, Charles   28, 166, 182
Marconi, Guglielmo   171

Margin Drive   85, 112, **120**, 133,
   167
Margin House   85, 120
Marlborough House   24, 28, 48,
   109, 149, 181, 182, 191
Marryat Place   11, 61, **121**, 170
Marryat Road   11, 23, 37, 60, 61,
   **121**, 133, 170
Marryat, Captain Frederick   121,
   132, 170
Marryat, Charlotte   11, 61, 63,
   121, *122*, 133, 183
Marryat, Joseph   11, 61, 121
Marsh, John   166, 167
Mason, Daniel   123
Mason, Mary, née Watney   83,
   123
Mason, Samuel   83, 97, 123, 182
Mason's Yard   97, **123**
McKay Road   47, 88, **123**
McKay, Alexander   123, 124
Melville Avenue   **124**, 161
Meyrick, James   137
Middleton, Admiral Charles, 1st
   Baron Barham   52
Milward, Richard   5, 15, 114, 146,
   157, 193
Moffat, William   149
Morley Park   41
Morley, Atkinson   11, 34, 51, 137
Mortlake, Manor of   17, 59, 96,
   148, 164
Morton, John, Archbishop of
   Canterbury   18, 139, 179, 190
Munthe, Axel   153
Munthe, Major Malcolm   153
Murray II, John   127
Murray III, John   102, 127
Murray Road   74, 94, **126**
Murray, Emily, née De Visme   126

200

201

Antonio, Duchess of Cannizaro 66, 182
Plunkett, John, 17th Baron of Dunsany 88
Plunkett-Ernle-Erle-Drax, Admiral the Honourable Sir Reginald 38, 47, 52, 63, 85, *87*, 89, 90, 91, 99, 110, 124, 136, 171, 185
Possil House 117
Preece, Sir William 171
Preston Road 37, 38, 47, **136**, 171
Prospect Place 77, 79, **136**, 139
Prospect Place estate 30, 32, 51, 79, 137, 183
Prospect Place House 25, *32*, 34, 70, 77, 105, 136, 181, 182, 183, 184, 191
Prosser, William 166
Putney Heath 36, 103, 134

Queen's Road 42
Queensmere Close **138**
Queensmere House 54, 144
Queensmere Lake *138*, 144, 184
Queensmere Road 9, **138**

Raynes Park Station 31, 32, 79, 184
Rectory Orchard 59, **139**, 169
Rhodes, Cecil 67
Ricards Lodge School 24
Richardson Evans Memorial Playing Fields 67
Richmond Park 67, 142, 143
Ridgway 2, 9, 17, 33, 34, 40, 61, 74, 77, 93, 94, 95, 103, 105, 113, 118, 130, 131, *141*, 143, 145, 150, 164, 169, 170, 171, 183, 184
Riley, Willie 168

Robin Hood Farm, Gate, Pub, Walk, Way & Well 142, 143
Robin Hood Road **142**, 155
Rockingham, Marquess of 27, 161, 181
Rocque, John 169
Rokeby Place 54, **143**
Rokeby School 12, 34, 143, 184
Rose & Crown, The, formerly The Sign of the Rose 23, 30, 83, 97, 123, 180, 182
Rounds, The *see* Caesar's Camp
Royal Close 12, 54, **144**
Royal Wimbledon Golf Club 39, 124, 184, 185
Rush, Martha 29, 181
Rushmere House 182, 191
Rushmere Place **144**
Rushmere Pond 42, 145
Rydon Mews 39, 70, **145**
Rydon, Lieutenant Colonel HJ 11, 145

Sawbridge-Erle-Drax, John Samuel Wanley 16, 36, 38, 63, *64*, 89, 111, 184
School Lane *see* Camp Road
Schwann, John Frederick, subsequently Swann 129
Schwann, Margaret Anne, née Holland 129
Scott, Sir George Gilbert 33, 149, 154, 183
Second World War 38, 52, 62, 89, 93, 94, 102, 107, 113, 129, 135, 144, 153, 164
Selassie, Haile, Emperor of Ethiopia 67, 116
Selfridge, Rosalie, later Princess Wiasemsky 151, 152
Seligman family 116, 117

203

# ABOUT THE AUTHOR

Neal Ransome has lived in Wimbledon since 1968. He went to King's College School, Wimbledon and read Modern History at New College, Oxford. He was for many years a corporate finance partner at PwC, and is now a non-executive director of two companies and a trustee of the RSPB, the UK's largest nature conservation charity. Neal is married to Patricia, a specialist teacher, and has three adult daughters. He is a member of The Wimbledon Society Local History Group. This is his first book.

## Dedication

This book is dedicated to my parents, Peter and Hazel Ransome.